a PRIESTHOOD
imprisoned
A Crisis for the Church

John E. Ryan

Coventry Press

Published in Australia by
Coventry Press
33 Scoresby Road
Bayswater Vic. 3153
Australia

ISBN 9780648145714

Copyright © John E. Ryan 2017

All rights reserved. Other than for the purposes and subject to the conditions prescribed under the Copyright Act, no part of this publication may be reproduced, stored in a retrieval system, or transmitted in any form or by any means, electronic, mechanical, photocopying, recording or otherwise, without the prior permission of the publisher.

First published 2017

Cataloguing-in-Publication entry is available from the National Library of Australia http:/catalogue.nla.gov.au/.

Cover concept by Jeanine Doyle
Design by Filmshot Graphics (FSG)

Printed in Australia

Contents

Dedication 5

Preface 7

A personal introduction 13

Chapter One
What ails us? 15

Chapter Two
Understanding how persons grow 27

Chapter Three
How we relate to God 43

Chapter Four
Concerning sexuality 61

Chapter Five
The issue of leadership 69

Chapter Six
Making moral choices 81

Epilogue 107

Appendix 1
The experience of being a priest in Australia today 109

Appendix 2
A final reflection 121

Dedication

This particular work is humbly dedicated to my brother priests, the men and women religious and the laity within our Church community, as we encounter the current purgation and search for wisdom and enlightenment.

When the abuse crisis first came to public attention in the early 2000s, I believe that the first response was to seek an explanation in certain "rotten apples" that had found their way into our midst. Later, there was a move to widen the explanation to include the inappropriate way the problem had been handled by those in authority. While both of these explanations were unsatisfactory, those in authority could hope for a cure within the confines of the existing structures. From the very beginning, I have been dissatisfied with both of these responses due to my belief that the perpetrators - many of whom were my brothers in the priesthood - were themselves not helped by a dysfunctional system. It is this systemic dysfunction that this work sets out to address.

Acknowledgments

I gladly acknowledge those friends who have contributed to the book at various stages of its development:

Dr Marie Keenan for her ongoing affirmation and encouragement, and the way her generous Preface has captured the message I have dared to share.

Fr Patrick Lim for the original set up and design.

Brian Morgan, a long-time school friend, for the photographs

Jeanine Doyle for the cover concept.

Fr John McKinnon and Michael Jarvis for their advice in the development and writing.

Teena Kell and Lorraine Smith for help in preparing the manuscript.

I apologise for being unable to spend more time and energy unpacking this message. God willing, slow and reflective reading will help to make up for my inadequacies.

Preface

When I wrote *Child Sexual Abuse and the Catholic Church: Gender, Power and Organizational Culture* (OUP, 2012), in which I proffered a systemic explanation for the problem of child sexual abuse in the Catholic Church, I sincerely hoped that it would encourage others, especially those with 'insider knowledge' and experience to elaborate what I could only begin to suggest. I am so delighted to see that this is what Fr John Ryan has done in this wonderful monograph, so aptly titled *Priesthood Imprisoned*. Dissatisfied with the explanations for and responses to the problem of child sexual abuse in the Catholic Church since the early 2000s, from the "rotten apples" theory of infiltrating offenders to the "cover up" theory of incompetent or dishonest bishops, Fr John set out to examine the issue for himself.

We arrive at the same spot, from my perspective after a decade of research and involvement with the key actors, and from Fr John's perspective after a lifetime as a Catholic priest: this is not a problem of individuals – of bad priests or bad bishops– this is a systemic problem of seismic proportions that no amount of individual blaming will solve. To understand and respond adequately and accurately to this problem it must be fully understood. For Fr John, the responses to date have been premised on a fundamental individualistic explanatory error while those in authority hope for a cure to be developed within the confines of the existing structures. Systemic problems require systemic solutions[1] and it is "the systemic dysfunction" that Fr John sees as underpinning child sexual abuse by Catholic clergy that this monograph sets out to address. This is a laudable

---

[1] *We both also acknowledge that individual wrongdoing requires individual accountability.*

task by an inspiring and wise author. One of the casualties of this systemic dysfunction is "a priesthood imprisoned". Clearly, another is the innocence of children who have suffered child sexual abuse at the hands of some.

I found the first part of the book *What Ails Us?* to be well charted and comprehensive in its focus on understanding and identifying the needs of priests. By offering the reader a summary of existing research and explanatory typologies and models to try to explain some of the current crisis in priesthood today, we are well on our way to seeing where Fr John is going: emotionally unhealthy and disregarded clerics who are not sufficiently equipped for the challenges of priestly ministry are at risk of working against the work of Love to which they have been ordained. By combining his knowledge of research on Catholic priesthood with his observations of priesthood in the Catholic Church and applying psychological theories of development to this work, Fr John comes to an important conclusion: that a sizeable number of priests in the Catholic Church are immature and incapable of forming healthy relationships without help. Unfortunately, I came to the same conclusion myself. Unable to form healthy relationships, these men will engage in unhealthy ones – and even engage in relationships of an abusive nature, unfortunately including the abuse of children. He and I see this to have been part of the jig-saw puzzle that created the context in which sexual abuse by Catholic clergy became possible. However, this factor alone is insufficient to fully explain the problem.

Ever persistent in his quest to examine the puzzle, Fr John moves into the realm of spirituality and works in a most readable fashion through the proliferation of theories that help us make sense of the complexity of our life's experiences. He considers categories and approaches to spirituality that can provide strength and others that can leave us vulnerable. Noting that

Christians have always sought maps and categories to help in their understanding of life with God, he suggests that it was mainly the philosophers and the spiritual masters in times gone by who provided this service, which is now so well served (or in my view not so well served) by the modern disciplines of psychology and psychiatry. Observing that not all of us are equally proficient in the spiritual life, Fr John unpacks some of the insights he personally gained through using what he likes to refer to as his three-stage PIU model of spirituality - The Purgative, Illuminative, Unitive Model [PIU] - to take us into some personally reflective depths. The PIU model is helpful and elaborated beautifully in this text– aided by the interweaving of the personal testimony and 'conversion' journey of Fr John himself. This was a moving feature of the entire monograph, which I suggest is essential reading for all Catholic clergy.

Going deeper into the question of spirituality in the section of the book, *How we relate to God,* I was persuaded by the claim that "the institutional processes of education and formation in the Catholic Church are frozen at immature stages of maturity which rely too much on fear, law and order and control and deprive too many of the experience of Christianity as Love" (p. 43). What an unfortunate situation the Catholic Church has allowed develop! However, in offering suggestions on how to find a way through to the central issue of any spirituality - which is the place it gives to God, to ourselves, and to the relationship between the two - I very much like Fr John's illumination of two models for a common spirituality (A and B) and his depictions of these perspectives as part of a spiritual continuum. I believe this section of the book, which is enhanced by the threads of transition and conversion through each line, will be enormously helpful to readers who want to reflect on their own spiritual life. Little condemnation is in sight in these pages. Rather, the wise, reflective, faith-filled and scholarly ideas of a life of reflective and challenging priesthood are eloquently and humbly portrayed and interwoven with the research on the topic: a constant feature of this most wonderful work.

While Fr John suggests that the topic of sexuality is such as to deserve a separate treatment all together, and what he offers is merely indicative rather than adequate, from my perspective his treatise of sexuality is well done and the questioning, even critical, approach adopted to Church teaching is significant, emanating from one who represents the lived experience. The honest appraisal of the lack of work on sexuality in the Bible is also significant and opens up this whole area for serious and honest discussion, from which Fr John does not retreat. The honesty of the discussion will be helpful for opening pathways for discussion among other Catholic clergy as they try to live within the complexity [and strengths, limitations and flaws] of Church teaching on sexuality today.

In order to establish a context for his discussion on leadership in the church, Fr John draws on a quote of Alexander Solzhenitsyn from a Harvard address, delivered in 1978, which helps him reassure readers of his belief that the problems in leadership and governance in the Catholic Church are not confined to that institution, but are endemic in all the basic structures of the Western world. The quote from Alexander Solzhenitsyn is fitting and sets the tone for this entire section. In addition, by drawing strongly on Gospel values and the New Testament, Fr John offers a perspective that can certainly aid contemporary thinking on the topic. Power and authority are not ignored but rather are examined with a critical eye, with the recent documentation from the Magisterium "that all stops are out to reverse any aberrations in the use of power" welcomed, but with a considered caution: "the new models will not survive unless we put them into new wineskins… We are not just being given new ideas or gimmicks: we are being called to *metanoia*, which is a change of mind and heart... It demands a whole change of values" (p. 76). I cannot disagree with a single argument offered by Fr John in his work on power and authority in the church.

In presenting his treatise of guilt, the superego and healthy conscience, Fr John's suggests a template for considering our moral world - one ruled by superego and another by healthy conscience. In applying this template to seminary formation, the view of Fr John that people who have been the object of moral "training" rather than moral "education" – what I call a rule-based morality rather than a relational ethic - will encounter particular difficulty in life, goes right to the heart of the matter. Returning again to the Gospel for guidance, he further suggests "For the Gospel, the external is secondary; the important element is the heart. The Beatitudes are 'be-attitudes', and call for being as the basis for doing. The institutionalised model is built up almost exclusively from a consideration of externals or visibles and is prone to a legalistic approach" (p. 69). This emphasis on 'the heart' and the 'be' of the Beatitudes which he further develops hold promise for charting a way forward for seminary formation.

In offering some helpful suggestions for a way forward for the Imprisoned Priesthood, Fr John rather challengingly reminds that "there are two ways of leaving priesthood: one is to leave and move out, the other is to leave and stay in!" (p. 95). He offers pointers for those who want to leave and stay in... I think like himself. In my view, the only way forward for a healthy life for those who wish to remain in the Catholic priesthood is to leave (the old) and stay in (and create the new). Fr John offers wise guidance on this, with affectivity and mercy key considerations.

This is a wonderful and exciting monograph that brings together much interesting material in a most helpful, warm, wise and innovative way. It will be of benefit to many priests throughout the world – especially those in personal trouble – and will be of interest to the laity and those interested in understanding Catholic priesthood and the Catholic Church. The writing style is warm, personal and accessible, with a depth of scholarship and wisdom. I feel like I know Fr John, having read this incredible, moving and wise document. It has been a real privilege and I am humbly honoured to endorse the work.

Marie Keenan
University College Dublin

A Personal Introduction

As a priest ordained in 1963, I have had a keen interest in the Christian life and in my priesthood in particular from the very beginning. I took seriously the eight years of seminary training and when I took up my first parish appointment believed I had the answers I would need for my life ministry or at least knew where and how to find them.

On the occasion of our twenty-five years anniversary of ordination Mass, I was invited to deliver the homily where I tried to spell out the story of those beginning years. Briefly, I described receiving a well secured and presented priesthood into our newly consecrated hands in 1963 only to find that almost at once the seals began to rupture and the content began to leak out. Those first twenty-five years I described as a challenging journey to rediscover what our priesthood involved and how to reclaim it anew. I confidently claimed that we had rediscovered it as a call to follow Jesus as disciples and would spend our next twenty-five years searching for how to do this in the various changing situations we would find ourselves. As I look back now, that daring prediction of 1988 has proved to have the ring of prophecy to it. My life as a priest has indeed been a life of continuous questioning and searching and a great part of this in professionally structured fellowship with my brother priests.

In the aftermath of Vatican II, it soon became clear that a new world was dawning within the Church. Religious orders and lay groups were organising themselves in various ways to understand and adapt themselves to the "promising new outpouring of the Spirit". Priests, especially diocesan priests, were feeling left out and began to organise themselves to do something about it. From more informal gatherings at the Hume Weir outside of

Albury which eventually evolved to become the NCP or National Council of Priests, to meetings of those with a more formal responsibility to care for their brother priests, a more committed group formed with the specific intention of doing something to serve the need for the ongoing renewal of priests here in Australia. That group became known as AAPROCC [Australian Association for Pastoral Renewal of Catholic Clergy], and for some time they searched to find someone who could do the necessary work of converting a worthy dream into some form of reality. Fortuitously, in 1980, I was finishing a term where I had been engaged with David Walker in establishing the Educational Centre for Christian Spirituality in Randwick and was approached by that entrepreneurial genius Eric Hodgens, the man then heading up AAPROC, to give some time to realise their dream.

As they say, the rest is history and led in turn to my being involved with the founding of the St Peter Centre, the Ministry for Priests Program, the Catholic Institute for Ministry and the Humanita Foundation for the Study of Christian Sexuality - in short, a life-time involvement at home and abroad with Christian Education and Formation for priests and laity. During this time, it has been my privilege to search with countless men and women of exceptional knowledge, wisdom and sanctity and it is from this source that I dare to share whatever I can for this current project. Whatever is helpful and true will have been found in and through them; whatever is confused and likely to get in the way of love and life, I must take responsibility for and I do.

Chapter One

What Ails Us?

Integral to any attempt to respond to the expressed needs of our brother priests was the task of identifying what those needs might be. How to do this was our first challenge and it was my utter conviction that the prime source of what we wanted was in the hearts and dreams of the men themselves. For longer than I could remember, I have been tantalised by the message *"I will place my law within them, and write it upon their hearts"* [Jeremiah: 31:33. Hebrews: 10:16]. I had a concern that too often our 'education and formation' processes overloaded us, even oppressed us and I was keen to ensure that attempting to meet the genuine needs of those we set out to serve would be our primary goal, and that only those who were personally enlivened by what they had to share would be invited to work in our programs. I sincerely believe that when we were able to keep to that goal, we were successful! I was especially empowered with the response of Jesus to the blind man who came to him seeking help. Jesus said to him, "What would you have me to do for you?" Here was the place to begin.

Alongside of what could be learnt from dialogue with individual priests, there was a sizeable store of findings available within our tradition and from various more recent researchers in the field of developmental psychology. In passing, it is worth noting that as far as official Church data was concerned, there was a cloud of suspicion arising from the unprofessional censuring of certain lines of inquiry by the authorities and their lack of openness to accept certain answers. Such censorship was particularly irksome whenever traditional practices such as mandatory celibacy and blind obedience were called into question.

By 1981, when the St Peter Centre opened its doors in Canberra for the first time, we had what we believed to be a working profile of our priestly clientele that suggested that some twenty per cent were well adjusted, mature and generally able to handle their current and ongoing needs. These men could provide a sound resource in any renewal work that might be required and in fact many of them did so and in magnificent ways! Another twenty per cent showed signs of a need for professional mental and/or emotional attention. The major sixty per cent while seemingly coping would need some organised help if they were to adjust adequately to the challenges of modern priesthood. This working profile was behind all the initial planning and was added to and modified progressively as we went forward. By way of unpacking this view, let me share some of the contributing research data.

Early Research

1. Prior to the 1971 Synod of Bishops which considered The Ministerial Priesthood, along with the topic of Justice in The World, the Dutch psychiatrists Conrad Baars and Anne Terruwe presented the results of their extensive clinical observations of priests. Prefacing their presentation with the general claim "that the emotional and spiritual growth of people today has not kept pace with their physical and intellectual growth", they went on to claim that of all priests in Western Europe and North America: 10-15% were mature, 20-25% had serious psychiatric difficulties, 60-70% suffered from a degree of emotional immaturity that did not prevent them from exercising their priestly function, but precluded them from being happy men and effective priests whose fundamental role was to bring people the joy of Christ's love

and to be the appropriate affirmers of others. They noted, "We have been advised by Vatican observers of the crisis in the entire World Church that there is a remarkable agreement between their statistics and our own percentages".

2. Another study by Fr Eugene Kennedy and Dr Victor Heckler commissioned in 1971 by the National Conference of Catholic Bishops in the U.S.A., and using different criteria from that used by Baars and Terruwe, measured the emotional development of priests and found that: 7.01% are emotionally developed, 18.45% were developing, 66.05% were underdeveloped and 8.48% were maldeveloped. Clearly, they found that a large proportion of priests were emotionally underdeveloped and immature and that such incomplete personal development results in distant, unrewarding relationships and uneasiness about intimacy, with resulting difficulties with one's personal identity, non-integrated psycho-sexual identity, and lack of self-confidence.

3. In 1984, the Australian Catholic Bishops Conference invited the American based The Center for Human Development [CHD] to launch their Ministry to Priests Program here in Australia. Over four years, 1985-88, more than 1300 priests, mainly diocesan, from sixteen of the dioceses and archdioceses of the country, answered a series of questionnaires designed to measure their personal attitudes and capabilities. In a composite report produced by The Center in 1989, they stated, "Although holism and personal integration may be the ideal of the Australian priests, the statistics contained in the study indicate that those ideals are seldom achieved. The statistics contained in this study, when compared to the population reflected in the total statistical analysis available through CHD, indicate that the Australian priests function below average in areas of personal emotion, maturity, expression of self through interpersonal relationships, and

moral integrative achievement. They function at an above-average capacity, however, regarding traditional theological and spiritual concepts."

4. In 1990, Fr John McKinnon reviewed *The Profile of the Priests of Australia* which was prepared by The Center for Human Development in 1989 and produced *A Closer Look At Australian Priests*. Though the data considered by McKinnon had been gathered using instruments devised by more recent developmental psychologists, his summary produced a remarkably consistent profile; namely of a group of men who were emotionally underdeveloped and hindered in their ability to relate creatively. But let his comments speak for themselves. He first reported on the findings from the Washington University Sentence Completion Test of Ego Development devised by Dr Jane Loevinger. This test measured respondents according to three levels of personal growth: the conformist, the conscientious and the autonomous. From the data provided by this test, McKinnon commented, "Sadly, according to the criteria used in this test, only about one in ten [9%] of the priests in the sample have comfortably and consistently reached a high level of human maturity where they each think for themselves and take note of their feelings... and approach moral behavior on the basis of their appreciation of the values involved".

Reflecting further on the data, McKinnon went on to say, "While the Conformist person is concerned with obedience to rules and regulations, those at the Conscientious level begin to experience conflict between law and personal needs. The Autonomous /Integrated person can move, when appropriate, with maturity and responsibility beyond the law to the Church's traditional teaching that all laws are based on love." Only 1 in 10 priests have reached this high level of human maturity; and research in America some years ago suggested that the Church was apparently not a benign environment for such men!

He noted that those priests who seem unquestioningly and uncritically to accept the institution they serve are twice as many as in the population at large. Their obedience is not a mature obedience and is a cause of personal stress.

While 84% see God as source of love and freedom, there is a noticeable inconsistency in that up to 66% of priests have difficulty in being in touch with their feelings!

A Closer Look At Australian Priests

Conformist & Conformist-Transitional 35%

- *concerned with roles, rules and regulations*
- *loyal, obedient, 'followers rather than leaders'*
- *largely unaware of the distinction between inner life and external actions*
- *perceive themselves and others as conforming to traditional norms*
- *insensitive to individual differences*
- *tension experienced when faced with breaking a rule or stepping outside accustomed role*
- *compassion bows to orthodoxy*

Conscientious & Conscientious-Transitional 56%

- *can differentiate morality from custom*
- *aware of inner needs and feelings*
- *able to distinguish between inner life and external actions*
- *more open to complexity, differences and exceptions*
- *accepts others as individuals*
- *tension results from conflict between law and personal needs and from the fear of, and desire to control, newly discovered inner feelings, warmth and spontaneity.*

Autonomous & Integrated 9%
- *chooses person/love ethics and acts responsibly in moving beyond rules*
- *not over-dependent on authority*
- *responsible for own life and willing to accord the same right to others*
- *accepts tension and conflict as necessary for human growth and seeks to reconcile polarities rather than eliminating one of them, e.g.: mind/ body, intellect/ emotion, conscience/ law, needs of self/ demands of others, spontaneity/ control.*

Significant Corroborative Testimony

Before concluding this attempt to provide a profile of our priests that would support a claim of institutional systemic dysfunction, let me share a couple of flesh and blood testimonies.

1. In 1995, the Consultant Psychologist Bryan M. Gray was asked to comment on "the symptoms of pain and hope" that the Diocesan Directors of Continuing Priestly Education had identified in their 1993 and 1994 conferences. He wrote: "I thought that these various symptoms were associated with helplessness, inadequacy and depression and pointed to an underlying sense of impotence that may be experienced by a number of priests today. In a number of instances discussed, this impotence was associated with states of 'emotional dependence' on church and societal authorities. It also heightened feelings of frustration and intensified the powerlessness. This profound pain sometimes reached pathological proportions and expressed itself in forms of abuse [sexual, alcoholic, corruption, etc.]". Gray went on to say, "These thoughts lead me to formulate two key questions: How would one leave or separate from such states of 'emotional dependence' and become more able to take roles and authority as a priest in relation to others in church and society? What kinds of educative and formative processes would assist such change?"

2. Prior to his untimely death in 2006, Monsignor Joe Rheinberger of the Archdiocese of Canberra and Goulburn, who did so much in service of his brother priests and who incarnated in his own life story the thesis of this work, wrote the following testimony: "Human growth is possible. It belongs to the dynamic of God's grace. But no one can make an individual grow, not even God. Because all growth is an adventure in freedom, it is inseparably tied into an individual's

own decision. I was brought up in a Church which cherished the will and intellect. We had a theology that was saturated with reason and law, and even now we are expected to submit our mind and will in obedience to authority. All this made affinity with love somewhat difficult. Not that love does not need reason, will, discipline and rationality, but the roots of love were learned in our childhood when feelings were predominant and were the main means of conveying affection to us. We are steeped in the signals and symbols of feelings, and we cannot be effective lovers without a major use of feelings. It has become axiomatic that having a sense of control over one's life, a sense of ownership and participation, is basic to morale and maturity. Closely related to ownership and participation is the need for a sense of community, common vision and mutual responsibility. It is devastating to morale for priests to feel isolated from one another, not understood by superiors and left alone before criticism and complaint. Love of self is important for all Christians, but the priest in particular. [How do we grow as people who relate closely and well? How do we assess and meet our personal needs?] It is not easy to be constantly available to others without recharging one's own batteries. Authentic love of self allows us to recharge our batteries without any sense of guilt and makes it possible to continue to love others without resentment."

3. In their 2011 book, *Our Fathers - What Australian Catholic Priests Really Think About Their Lives And Their Church* (Mulgrave, Vic.: John Garratt Publishers), Chris McGillion and John O'Carroll noted: "The morale of priests is in urgent need of attention. [We found] ... much evidence to suggest a professional crisis in terms of the demands made on priests in their everyday parish ministry and the lack of support offered to them.

"Most priests report that they are extremely stretched by the workloads, feel marginalised from decision-making processes, and have little confidence in the direction in which those who do make the decisions are taking the Church in this country.

"While it [the Church] professes to respect the integrity of each individual, it appears to operate internally in ways little different to any other large-scale bureaucratic organisation in contemporary society. We came into contact with some priests whose loneliness was palpable, whose presbyteries left an unmistakable impression of gloom and neglect, whose offices were cluttered with religious paraphernalia that seemed to obscure entirely their own personalities, who had surprisingly little to say of any insight after many years of service to the Church, and who seemed to be spent of all energy and enthusiasm to do more than simply go through the motions until the uncertain years of their retirement.

"Generally, priests felt that bishops in this country were poor choices. Many priests went further in their depiction of the caliber of the bishops being chosen, expressing the view that appointments are now made not on the basis of talent but on fidelity to the hierarchy in Rome. No other topic in this study elicited quite the same strength of negative feeling than the quality of the relationships between priests and their bishops. The great difficulty that priests [65%] have in confronting their demons whatever their source leaves them an easy prey for incompetence."

Before leaving these remarks by McGillion and O'Carroll, let me say that while much of what they say might be interpreted as coming from a small number of 'odd bods', our data argues that the numbers are significant; and they are damning. I would also want to note the obvious lack of interest that has been shown in such an unhealthy situation. This is evidenced by the fact that studies such as these have been appearing with monotonous regularity, and no appreciable response seems to have been offered. The hope of the early 1980 appears to have dissipated.

4. One question has to be asked: Do the present faithful at large want their priests to mature? Research done elsewhere [Philip Hughes, 1989, *The Australian Clergy*, The Christian Research Association] indicates that the majority of Christians belong to a Church because they see it as a source of peace and a refuge from the stresses of the secular world. Many prefer a priest who does not challenge them and is content to leave them secure in the familiar and the unchanging. If the price of that is a priest who may be compassionate but falls short on intimacy, many of them seem to be content to pay the price. In a conformist Church, counseling more often than not reverts to advice along with the 'take it or leave it' tag, which is what most people are comfortable with. Whatever about this, clearly the Church as a whole needs a climate and structures that encourage and support human and spiritual growth, patterns of interacting and dialogue. The systemic problem I am striving to highlight obviously reverberates throughout the whole structure and nothing less than structural reform will do.

5. As far back as 1985, Fr David Coffey, speaking out of his long experience as a professor at St Patrick's College, Manly, claimed that "our kind of seminary can no longer function adequately as a place facilitating the formation process."

The relative failure of programs that set out to combine general priestly formation with attendance at adjacent universities is of particular interest and may well be connected with anecdotal evidence suggesting that candidates entering seminary formation programs regress rather than advance in terms of relational abilities and psychological maturity. Arguments that point to advances in psychological pre-testing of candidates and advances in psychological sensitivity in formation programs are of little relevance to my position that is primarily looking at past contributors to priestly abuse. This having been said, I would want to say that many, if not all, of the 'remedies' so far put forward in response to the current crisis have been conceived and born within the same systemic environment that has given rise to many of our present problems!

The above observations and evaluations of priesthood have come mainly from applying particular psychological theories of development to observations of priests in the Catholic Church. I believe that they validate the claim that a sizeable number of our priests are immature and incapable of forming healthy relationships without help.

To paraphrase a statement of St John of the Cross, I do not want to add any more references here on so clear a matter (A3,18,2). For those who want more, on Wednesday 28th 1984, the Australian Bishops in Conference met to explore the situation of the Australian priest. One paper presented at that time is of particular interest in identifying the condition of the priesthood at that time. I include an edited version of that paper as an appendix to this work.

Chapter Two

Understanding how persons grow

Developmental psychology is the scientific study of how and why human beings change over the course of their life. Originally concerned with infants and children, the field has expanded to include the whole lifespan. Jean-Jacques Rousseau is typically cited as one of the founders of modern developmental psychology. It is of particular interest to note that in the mid-18th century, Rousseau described three stages of development: infans, puer and adolescence. In the late 19th century, psychologists following Darwin began seeking an evolutionary description of development to match an evolutionary understanding of human growth that stood in opposition to existing static models of understanding. I have seen claims that there is presently something like two dozen credible theories of human development associated with names like Piaget, Erickson, Kohlberg, Maslow, Loevinger, Gilligan, Fowler, Levinson, Keegan and Wilber. In various ways, all of these seek to chart how life's journey unfolds. While the theories differ for various reasons, I find an interesting similarity amongst them.

Human Complexity

The proliferation of these theories indicates that they provide a valuable service in helping to make sense of the complexity of life's experience. They can be good 'models for' understanding and give a language with which we can begin to communicate about life's experiences. Along with the popularity of development theories, there is the skepticism of those who feel that here again we are in an area where people are claiming an indecent amount of knowledge, and worse still, daring to act on it. As in most disputes, the fertile ground is probably between the two extremes. When we approach the human person, we come into the presence of an individual complexity that is ultimately a mystery that cannot be fully grasped or understood by us. However, through the power of imagination, we are able to find analogues or pictures that are available to our experience and that can stand alongside our mystery and mirror something of it to us. Such analogues are known as models and there will be many of them, depending on the angle from which the mystery is approached and the particular theory we have adopted to understand it.

Models

Personally, it always helps me to note that I am dealing with analogues or models that assist my approach to matters of mystery. When they work, they put me in touch, but never can they bring me close enough to capture the experience or put me in complete control. The temptation is always there for me to treat them as 'models of' understanding, rather than 'models for'; whenever I succumb to such a temptation I am in danger of trying to adjust the experience to fit the model. Even now, I react regularly whenever I hear someone referred to as a number on the Enneagram or as a combination of letters according to the Myers-Briggs model! Perhaps the worst example of falling for this temptation was the case of a religious congregation where all of the members were identified according to their readings on the Enneagram!

I recall with affection the words of a dear friend and saintly psychiatrist, Dr Eric Seal, who acknowledged the value of the various models yet constantly reminded us that we must never lose sight of the wonderfully serendipitous nature of life. In a book review in the 80s, Jonathan D. Foster wrote in *Review for Religious*, "Bernice Neugarten, doyenne of developmental researchers at the University of Chicago for three decades, used to say that after all the research and all the distinctions, all we really know about adult development is that there is some. It is a disservice not to pass on to the uninitiated the tentative character of these findings."

Given these reservations, I must say that I have been well served at different times by each of the various models that I have come across. All of them have a value and provide something of a window through which to peep into the mystery of life. They are more indicative and suggestive than descriptive, more poetic than definitive, yet extremely useful.

Earlier Models

The newfound, or better, newly recovered sensitivity to the inner life and its transitions is not a discovery of something never known before. Ancient wisdom was well aware of this process of change and evolution leading to different stages of life and ways of living. What is truly fascinating is the similar outcomes coming from the many studies both old and new.

From earliest times in Christian history, people have sought map-like categories to help them negotiate the journey of life with God. Nor is it surprising that they would model their maps on the natural way that life seems to evolve. I suspect that until recently it was mainly the philosophers and the spiritual masters who provided this service, which is now so well served by the modern disciplines of psychology and psychiatry. The growing popular awareness of human life as a journey marked by crucial stages of personal development has flourished in recent years.

In the second century, we find St Clement of Alexandria [150-215] classifying people as 'children, men and the wise and initiated' [whom he called Gnostics]. St Gregory of

Nyssa [330-395] saw people living in stages of fear, hope or charity; Cassian [360-435] had a similar scheme. Both Sts Augustine [354-430] and Bernard [1090-1153] opted for models built on degrees of love, while St Thomas Aquinas [1225-1274] held to the model of childhood to adulthood, and focused on the effects of charity present in a person's life. In her *Dialogue*, St Catherine of Siena [1333-1380] had a fascinating model based on her understanding of how the disciples lived with the Lord before Calvary, from Calvary to Pentecost, and after Pentecost.

In his inspiring book *God of Surprises*, Gerard W. Hughes gives a valuable presentation of Baron Von Hugel's model. Von Hugel saw people moving from spiritual childhood to adolescence and onto maturity. Once again, these few references are no more than a representative sample!

It is obvious that all of us are not equally proficient in the spiritual life. So there arises the question as to whether or not there are stages through which God usually leads people. Since the time of the Fathers, it has been usual to distinguish three specific stages in the journey towards spiritual wholeness. Sometimes these stages are further sub-divided and often the way that one is to live within each of the stages is spelt out too and we have 'ways' referred to as well as stages. The recurring triptych of the purgative, illuminative and unitive ways seems to go back in Christian history at least to Evagrius Ponticus [346-99] and is subsequently picked up and used by various writers down to our own time.

The Purgative, Illuminative, Unitive Model [PIU]

Allow me to be personal in presenting this section. At different times I find myself taking up one or other of the available models depending on the circumstances I am trying to make sense of.

Overall, I would say that my preferred model is an adapted form of the traditional Purgative, Illuminative and Unitive (PIU) triptych. I say 'adapted' because, in applying the models to our own unique circumstances, we inevitably and necessarily tailor them. I believe that it is this tailoring which explains why we rarely, if ever, find two commentators talking of the models in exactly the same way.

Let me unpack some of the insights I gain through using what, for convenience, I like to refer to as my PIU model. Against the background of this model, I see my life as falling into three rather distinct phases.

1. The Purgative Phase

This phase takes me up to and into my years of ordained priesthood when my predominant concern was to find out what was expected of me. In many ways, this was a time of living by the rules, seeking acceptance by conformity or following the Lord as the Way [John 14:6]. Reward and punishment were main motivators. The purgative phase is a kind of socialising phase where we strive to get our behaviour to conform to that of the group and the virtue is to obey those who have a position of authority over us. The sense of feeling good is important.

Transition

A convergence of factors such as the experience of ineffectiveness in recommended practices, lack of satisfaction in ministry and decreased credibility of those in authority led me to see the limitations of this first or 'purgative way' and sent me on to the next phase of my journey.

2. The Illuminative Phase

Here I was involved in a search for meaning, to understand what it was all about. For me the 'illuminative phase' is about vision and understanding and value; no longer just the *what* and the *how* but also the *why* of it all. Here I see myself seeking to follow the Lord as the Truth! Interestingly, as often happens, this phase of my life's journey also involved me in an extensive and long-lasting geographical pilgrimage. There was a special intensity to this stage that might well be due to my highly developed inquisitive nature. This was the era that saw me deeply addicted to what I now see as the 'drug of academe'. It was also the time when I developed many of my models of understanding that gave meaning to life. However, I did not always appreciate the essential relativity of the models or theologies I came up with and tended to give them a degree of absoluteness or infallibility that they could not sustain. I guess you could say that I was basically blind to my now-favourite distinction between *models of* and *models for*.

Looking back, I suspect that in this phase I was not only addicted to getting to the truth of the matter. I was convinced that there could be only one way to express that truth once found. If you like, I was pretty much a *'one model'* person. I was following my Lord as the Truth, but **my** truth tended to be my 'god'. Of course, a prime motivator in all my endeavors was my search for power and control.

Transition

When I look to identify the process that led me on from this state, I recall how a couple of sayings of an eccentric Marist Brother began to rise up again in my memory. He used to say, "There were more ways to kill a cat than drowning it in milk", and "To every rule there was an exception, even to that rule, for some rules don't have exceptions"! Maybe it was such a reawakening of consciousness and an appreciation of intuition that brought an end to these invigorating years of my salvation by knowledge. I remember how I came to be mesmerised by Simone Weil's statement that truth was the point where opposites could sit together!

Then too, I had moved to mid-life and - with a new force - had come up against questions of intimacy and relationships. For me it was impossible to relate to the wonderful people around me without realising that I did not have the monopoly on truth, and that there was much more to life than having the right formula or the right understanding. I was confronted by the impracticability of needing to have tailored answers to many of the questions of life and I came to realise, with the help of a special friend, how dogmatic and legalistic I had become.

These were some of the elements that helped me see how my world-view that had promised power and understanding was now moving away from being a life-giving haven towards being another crippling prison. I was readily reminded of the way our ancestors had experienced 'Egypt' as a place of life and liberty only later to experience it as a place of slavery. Like our ancestors, I needed to begin to experience the limitations of my former place of freedom to see it now as a place of slavery. Another conversion was coming and another journey would have to be made, maybe even geographically.

As one's journey unfolds, the process is catapulted from one stage to another by way of **conversion** involving the hallmark Christian pattern of dying and rising. St John of the Cross made famous two major transition phases, naming them as the 'dark night of the senses' and 'the dark night of the soul'. The mention of the Cross and the imagery of darkness are critical, and conversion is never easy. The Gospel warns that unless the grain falls into the ground and dies, it cannot bear fruit; while modern behavioural scientists are ready to remind us that there is no gain without pain! How often have the efforts to resist change and defend the "status quo", arising from fear and/or reluctance to face the challenge of conversion, caused me so much stress and strain in recent years?

Probing the Problem of 'Knowing'

Before I attempt to comment on the third stage of growth that one might expect to encounter on one's life journey, I need to say something about my experience of 'knowing', my experience of what one can know and how one knows. In those early years of confidence following ordination, my belief was that my 'knowledge' was capable of encompassing anything that I might need to know. I presumed there was an answer for everything somewhere, and it could be found in some form of intellectual proposition or statement, and it was available through intelligence and/or the voice of authority! When, as I described, that tidy way of life, and in particular priesthood, imploded dramatically in my early years in parish ministry, the issue of what I could know and how I could know became central and determined the shape of my personal search from that moment forward. Even today I can find myself shackled by the impact of this early naiveté which placed me in such an impoverished situation. As I look back now on my history, I see clearly that it was this same search to pursue the all-important question of knowledge that took me to study in Rome and onto the Jesuit university of St Louis. These years of study abroad were difficult and yet times of special grace and blessings.

The philosophical basis for my understanding of knowing had been firmly based in the worldview that had been adapted and built upon by the Scholastics, and in our day the Neo-Scholastics, who were focused on defending the old ways of seeing things against the modernising influence flowing from the Renaissance.

We were still cemented into the categories of the greatest of the Christian philosophers, St Thomas Aquinas [1225-1274], who used the ideas of Aristotle to discuss the existence and nature of reality. Though Duns Scotus [1266-1308] and the others were concerned with how we know things, the great French thinker René Descartes [1596-1656] was the first to discuss in detail how we know and what we know. From that time on, while the world of philosophy struggled with this issue of knowing - with people like Hume, Kant, Hegel, Bergson, Heidegger and Wittgenstein, tackling the questions that were being thrown to the surface by the new world - we as seminarians and priests remained buried in the basics of scholasticism struggling to remain relevant. Our exposure to those who were exploring the issues of modernity was to regard them as opponents or adversaries! Currently we are left with an incredible backlog of unattended questions as we face the task of catch-up.

3. The Unitive Phase

Relationship

For myself, the first painful breakthrough came as I slowly moved to appreciate that knowing/ knowledge was more than just an intellectual pursuit yielding to the application of reason. All too often, I have experienced the uselessness of a well-reasoned conclusion. A watershed moment came for me in the realisation that knowing was ultimately about relationship. This eventually led to my 2007 book *A Spirituality of Relationships – The Power of Both/And* (Richmond, Vic.: Spectrum 2007) Gradually it had become apparent to me that knowing was a gradual process, the richest form of which had to be understood in the biblical sense as a creative connection between the unknown and the knower. It was an episode in the advance of my appreciation that somehow ultimately all reality is connected and all is one! I had come to appreciate that 'knowing' is an experience that engages mind, emotions, behaviour, and social and spiritual aspects of my being. It is a growing and changing phenomenon. I was fascinated years ago hearing the renowned actress Shirley Maclaine reflecting on her hopes for the future. She wanted to continue to experience the move from information to knowledge, from knowledge to understanding and from understanding to wisdom. In an attractive way, she seemed to capture the mystery of it all.

Currently, I prefer concepts such as 'awareness' and 'consciousness' in trying to speak about the experiences previously gathered under the heading of 'knowing'. For me, I am painfully aware of the difficulty of communicating with you the reader when the relationship between us is so informal. Modern educators such as Parker Palmer and Sir Ken Robinson seem to be reinforcing my position when they stress the Gospel call to "do the truth in love".

I now see how, when propositions become the be-all-and-end-all of our knowing, I was trapped in a very primitive stage of awareness/consciousness and connectedness with the real world, and in danger of being imprisoned in a world of life-denying fantasy!

In the worldview that existed to my day and that held reign within our church culture, the connection with things gained through 'knowing' was achieved through the mind/intellect. As already noted true knowing engages the fullness of our reality – mind, heart, body, etc. I first awakened to the core of this phenomenon when during a concentrated period of studying religious experience, I became aware that it was a conglomerate of factors, intellectual/rational, emotional, social, spiritual and behavioural parts of our life. Tamper with any one aspect and the overall experience alters. It is this realisation that impacted on me and expanded gradually over the years that I cherish as one of the most important learnings of my life. It has led me to regret that I have not spent more of my educational efforts on developing my affectivity, my emotion, my social skills and my wider potential. It has also led me to embrace expressions I had previously referred to as knowing with words such as awareness and consciousness. These are words that I find in the writings of contemporary scholars who are engaged in studies of knowledge and love. Gaining a grasp of this new enlightenment has been difficult and taxing, and I see it as a big part of the conversion journey that moves us beyond the purgative and illuminative ways. Though I have never become a disciple of Bernard Lonergan, I have attended his lectures and I believe with others that he has tried to embrace this new vision of knowledge within the world of Neo-Scholasticism and in so doing has made a significant, if complicated, contribution to modern theology.

This third phase that is upon me still is well described as the 'unitive way', and as such it is about relationships and connecting. Here the issue is life, and living it to the full. Here the Lord is the Life. Here I can see the importance of the reality behind words such as holistic spirituality, community, dialogue, ecumenism and respect for the environment. As I look out over the new landscape that unfolds, I see a 'land of promise', marvellous beyond any words that I currently have at hand (Exodus 3:8).

The dominant force in this ongoing call to 'life and its fullness' is love which inhabits the universe and draws all that is, towards all that is. Like a sailor sailing on the sea and depending on the wind, one has to follow the pull to put oneself in the path of this power and be embraced in love. In the unitive way God is found as love and life.

Transition as Conversion

My PIU mode gives me a framework within which I can get a handle on my evolving life story. Over the years I've been struck by the number of developmental models that are made up of three basic stages or three groupings of stages. This is strikingly clear in the case of my PIU model, and it allows me to meaningfully position the two conversion stages: the Dark Night of the Senses and the Dark Night of the Soul made famous by St John of the Cross.

My first big conversion point came when I started to question the behavioural rules and regulations that I was trying to live up to. I needed to move on to understand the underlying principles and how God was calling me through them. Looking back, I see it as something like a movement from legalism to rationalism. It was at a time when authority and obedience were the main drivers in my life. From another point of view, I see that I had reached a stage where what I was doing no longer thrilled or satisfied me. In the phrase of *Annie's Song*, my lifestyle was no longer 'lighting up my senses!' From such a standpoint, it wasn't hard to understand this desert experience as a movement from the Purgative to the Illuminative Way and much of what the Tradition has to say about such an experience was helpful.

I was in my mid to late 30s as I crossed into this new land, and having experienced the agony and the ecstasy of this major conversion journey and finding my life settling into a stable and somewhat productive pattern, I thought that I had arrived at my journey's end. How naive can one be? Eventually *this* new land - my Egypt, if we are to keep in touch with the great archetypical story - slowly began to turn sour.

Interestingly, the time span during which I remained comfortably in the intellectually-dominated illuminative period before being led towards this present phase was somewhere between seven to ten years. When one starts to look at times or chronology, some of the age-related models, such as those in Daniel J. Levinson's book, *The Seasons Of A Man's Life*, come into their own; not to mention the mythology of the seven year itch! Such recollections are important in reminding us of the relationship between grace and nature and of St John of the Cross' claim that God leads us according to the mode of the receiver: that is God's grace is in conformity with the type of person we are.

As already noted, I believe that the coming of this second great conversion call was linked up with many things: the breaking open of the feminine within me, the need to receive as well as give, the tiredness and utter frustration of trying to save myself and sanctify myself through my achievements, and the realisation that no ethic, theology or ideology could satisfy my deepest urge which, like St Augustine's, was for relationship or union. Of course, this deepest urge is ultimately for God; and to the extent that love becomes increasingly purified and takes root in our life we become united with all reality at the base of which is God! Incidentally, the mention of Augustine recalls his *Confessions*, a fundamental text for all who seek to live a spiritual life and engage in the process of conversion.

Nowhere does the serendipitous nature of life show itself better than in relation to this conversion point which marks the threshold between the illuminative and the unitive stages; the so called 'dark night of the soul'. The opening out of life takes an uncanny twist. Till then it was as if I was going ahead pursuing life, now life seems to be coming in pursuit of me. How do we describe this? St Teresa of Avila describes this phenomenon of life coming after me, with a special clarity when she describes prayer using her metaphor of watering a garden. She speaks of drawing water in a bucket from a well, then diverting water from a stream near the garden, and finally by receiving a gentle rain from heaven. Clearly she is describing experiences that move from a focus on self-engagement to ever-higher receptivity. Interestingly Teresa was forty-seven years old when she wrote these words and well into her second conversion.

The psychiatrist Carl Jung referred to this exceptional turnaround in the way we experience the flow of life when he claimed that the second part of life needs to be negotiated according to coordinates other than those used in the first half! Years ago when I was privileged to work with alcoholics within the fellowship of Alcoholics Anonymous, I saw miracles happen on a regular basis when afflicted individuals dared to change their whole direction of life and to dare to 'let go and trust'. Experiences such as these convince me of a power that is available to us as humans and which is found in weakness more than strength. I believe that it is grace that we are talking of here which our Australian Bishops Conference rightly decided to focus on in 2012/2013 with the Year of Grace. Obviously, any work in this direction so far is little more than a beginning. Right here I need to acknowledge our painful ignorance of so much wisdom that is imbedded within the mystical traditions of various religious groups and which awaits the genuine searcher of whatever persuasion. Christianity is a mystic religion currently lost in a mire of moral rules and regulations. If we are to renew, then we need to re-find, to rediscover.

Maturity

Long ago, I found great comfort in Martin Marty's claim that Christianity is a religion for adults. Founded as Christianity is on a Trinitarian God who is Love, life for Christians is generated through creative bonding or love. Such love demands a special level of maturity that allows one to have a degree of ownership of one's life and the ability to enter into union with others and allow others in. In this context, our priestly profiles cry out an irrefutable message.

Whenever we are within the "spell of love", we are in the presence of a unifying force moving us from a singular reality outwards beyond ourselves, as we exist in the presence of true mystery. The Greek Fathers claimed the image of dancing to describe the interaction, or symbiotic-like state, where we are both giving and receiving at the same time. True mystery or grace is the realm of Christianity, and it requires a certain maturity which too many of us priests seemingly do not have! In categories made famous by Martin Buber, too many of us relate to fellow humans and to our world in objective-like 'I/It' couplings, not 'I/Thou' where there is a creative union in the meeting. Too often we are engaged with propositions or casuistry and blind to the presence of the personal.

In the purgative way, people's concern is for an objective reality outside of themselves that they have to obey: when they obey, there is a reward; when they fail, punishment. In the illuminative way, the concern is with particular understanding. The object of the purgative is an ethic, of the illuminative an ideology. When one enters into the unitive way, the big innovation which turns everything on its head is the engagement of the subject into the picture of reality one is dealing with. There is a lively interaction of the I-Thou, in contrast to the static immobility of the I-It encounter.

Losing nothing

In this general context, I need to stress that, just as the experiences of childhood and adolescence remain with one into adulthood, so too do the consciousness and the years of the purgative and the illuminative feed into the unitive until one's entire consciousness is transformed to see in all the face of God. As life progresses, the positive gains coming from earlier stages are not left behind but are caught up in the new stage and brought to a new richness. When one's consciousness is expanded and one is taken into the world of relationships, the gains of the years of law and order and the new understandings one gains along the way are incorporated and enriched in a new integration. How apt is the description of the scribe who draws out treasures both new and old [Matthew 13:52]?

How one talks about the mystic landscape is always a challenge and enforces the wisdom of the Gospel's call, "Come and see", for only those who are there will see, and their response will be to give thanks. The journey of life is to thanksgiving.

When, as I will claim, formation is aborted and limited to the controllable stages of the purgative and the illuminative ways, the mystery of life is denied and all kinds of repression results. To treat a person in such a way is without any doubt an abuse of one's charge.

Chapter Three

How we relate to God

Where I am heading in this presentation is to claim that the institutional processes of education and formation in our Church are frozen at immature stages of maturity which rely too much on fear, law and order and control, and deprive too many of the experience of Christianity as Love.

Above I have suggested that there are significant changes in the dynamic involved in the different stages of spiritual living. In stages one and two which I have described as the purgative and the illuminative, we are approaching an objective goal whereas with the unitive stage we are involved with the subjective, with relationships and the giving and receiving that is characteristic of them.

Several years ago, Val J. Peter wrote an article in the magazine *Review for Religious* [Vol 37, 1978/4, pp. 486–500] that described two different spiritualties that he saw existing within the ranks of regular Christians. I value this article as it helped me greatly at a time of real challenge. In the next few pages, I will rely heavily on this article. A central issue in any spirituality is the place it gives to God, to ourselves, and to the way of relating between the two.

Before we develop our own individual picture or blue print to live by [a task that belongs to adolescence or early adulthood], we live from the faith or life-picture of those around us. The picture or spirituality I grew up with arranged these major elements of life's jigsaw puzzle – God, self and my life style – into a very practical, clear and simple world-view. It gave me a clear understanding of God, of myself and the relationship between us. Above all, it gave me a rationale for how I was to behave and a clear basis for what I was to do. Like most things learnt in childhood, this spirituality has stayed with me over the years and only slowly have I come to see how it can be a mixture of good and bad! It contains the inevitable 'wheat and weeds' that characterise things of the Kingdom (Matthew 13:24-30).

Model A. Spirituality Focused on Behaviour

The central focus for me was on myself and my behaviour. I was given a list of doctrines and rules that I was told had been given to others by God and were now being handed onto me. While these doctrines and rules were portrayed as God's gift to me, deep down I often experienced them as oppressive and I regularly felt how much easier it was for the non-Catholics! This body of doctrines and rules stood before me as a group of ideas and behaviours, dogmas and ethics, if you like. They were the predominant consideration and my life vision was seen in terms of them. Believing and obeying them was the way in which I was to relate to God and God to me. My immediate focus really was not on God but on a list of things to do and not do, to accept and not accept. In their immediacy, they did mediate God to me in very tangible ways. However, the constant danger was that they could take the place of God and become predominantly an ideology or an ethic.

This did happen from time to time and it continues to happen in certain areas because, once planted, this vision still lingers on. I suspect that in early days this kind of spirituality worked well for me, especially when I was in a lively Christian community that shared that vision. Its potential weeds remained dormant until it came time to move on to a more mature mode. As I succumbed to the temptation to hang on to the past, my "Egypt" moved from being a place of support and nurture to becoming a place to escape the challenge to grow. In this particular spirituality, it was easy to miss the wood for the trees. Note again the value I find in the pilgrimage image of our ancestors in the faith and in particular the Passover from Egypt.

Evaluation

Let me briefly further unpack something of the ambiguity inherent in this kind of spirituality.

On the positive side

- It gave me the beginnings of a sense of identity by identifying acceptable ways of acting. It specified what good Christian boys were like.
- It gave a believable picture of God. God is very much like a good, wise human being who rewards good and punishes evil. God has a predetermined plan that is going to lead us to heaven; and if we fail to obey it, the whole human order will go haywire.
- What it said about religion was easy to understand, simple and clearly identifiable. What was required was also close enough to be achievable, and with the possibility of Confession it could be handled. I could seemingly obtain that peace we all yearn for and that the Gospel promises.
- By holding to the beliefs and keeping the rules, I was reassured by the fact that, when I did the right thing, God would be pleased and regard me favourably. 'All was well when I performed well.'

On the negative side

If we turn to examine the inherent 'weeds' or shortcomings of such a model of spirituality, its many dangers and pitfalls show up.

- It can trap one into experiencing self-worth in terms of performance. I am good and worthy because of what I do, not because of who I am in the image of God. Being locked into performance for one's worth will inevitably lead to a poor self-image.
- God is portrayed in very anthropomorphic terms and the sense of mystery can be lost. The God we know in this model can end up quite different from the God of Jesus who loves unconditionally and even seems to have a predilection for the spiritually poor and those who struggle with failure; in other words, the God who is Mercy. It is hard to approach the God of this model in one's weakness and amongst other things this discourages one from familial types of prayer where one's weaknesses and failures might be exposed.
- Religion can become something I do. The ascetical can take over and swamp the mystical – as has surely happened. Here it is indeed more blessed to give than to receive. Indeed, it is hard to experience grace as pure gift. Again we come back to the ever-present danger whereby religion and spirituality can deteriorate into little more than a code of ethical behaviours and/or an ideology.
- Perhaps the greatest danger of all is that it provides a real temptation towards self-righteousness. I found myself beginning to claim rights in the presence of God. When I had struggled and succeeded, I was no longer the unprofitable servant: God owed me! [Luke 17:10]. Abraham Maslow sees this as 'the divine right to be taken care of'. It can lead to great bitterness and selfishness in later life especially if, according to my categories, I feel that I have not been taken care of! Moreover, I can become very judgmental about others who do not shape up to the requirements as well as I do. 'If I can do it, so can they!' Smarting from the efforts needed for me to be good, I found myself drawn to deny rights of acceptance

to those who fail. At times, I could even go so far as to say that they deserved to be punished. I think it is this self-justification that Dietrich Bonhoeffer called the greatest of sins. Then, too, those who did not agree with my standards or beliefs become a special problem. My God had pretty much become identified with my moral code and belief system and I found myself reacting to those who disagreed with me with an energy that came from feeling that somehow my very life was threatened.

- While this model focuses very much on rules and behaviour, it can lead one to be selective in one's approach to the moral demands of the Gospel. Interestingly enough, our human need for abasement seems to lead us consciously to accept a list of demands that fall just outside our permanent capability; but not so far outside that some ritual such as Confession can't handle it. That was certainly how it was for me. A person living according to this model can treat the commandments like an end-of-term examination paper: 'Ten questions, choose two'. Interestingly, and well worthy of note, is the fact that the ones chosen will nearly always include obedience and sexuality! This phenomenon, whereby we cut our cloth according to our abilities, easily leads us to neglect or distort so much of the invitation of the Gospel. I recall vividly a question I once put to a prominent bishop regarding the obvious difference in importance he placed between the two encyclical letters of Pope Paul VI, *Populorum Progressio*, "On the Development of Peoples" and Humanae *Vitae*, "On Human Life". His reply was simply to inform me on how infamously inept Vatican sources were in the area of politics!

- God is seen very much in terms of an object, or as Martin Buber would say, in terms of the 'I/it' category. Grace too becomes an objective commodity that can be easily divided, measured and quantified. I see this approach to grace as

explaining the paralysing confusion that exists in one of the most important areas of theology dealing with the questions of merit, faith and free will.
- Finally, this kind of spirituality leads to an either/or interpretation of reality. Either I am in the 'good books' or I am not; in grace or in sin. 'How far can I go?' becomes a very real question and casuistry becomes the major concern of moralists. There's little place for the concept of daily conversion and development and gradual growth in virtue, and grace is not really catered for.
- It was as if my education were an exercise in my being moulded into a preconceived pattern rather than being led out and invited to be my unique self. It could and did give rise to 'educative' processes that were abusive.

Transition/Conversion

In many ways a spirituality such as this can serve us well in our immaturity as children, and in that context it can be appropriate. Its main problem for me is that it cannot handle the complexity of experiences that eventually come the way of *most* people as life strains to burst forth. Because of this inability to adjust to the complexities of life, one will either deny the experiences or jettison the spirituality, and with it God. Whether in fact it is a truly Christian model is debatable. I believe that for most people the invitation will eventually come to move on from this type of spirituality. The call to enter into such a conversion journey will normally come through a build-up of experiences that cannot be easily integrated into our existing framework. In some 'divinely unjust way', the more faithful one has been in living according to this early understanding, the more difficult the transition can be. If one fails to take the invitation to convert when it is offered, one will tend to stagnate or regress and then this kind of spirituality can become very dangerous and potentially destructive as the weeds gradually overtake the wheat. It did just that for me.

Model B
Spirituality Focused on Relationship with God

Reflecting as we are on our understanding and practice of spirituality is another way of examining our ideas of holiness. Some scholars would claim that our ideas of holiness are the most important formative influence on our lives, greater even than our notions of God. Personally, I am inclined to agree with them. If the Model A of spirituality described above depicts a position at one end of a hypothetical spirituality continuum, we might describe the position at the other end in the following way.

In the earlier model, behaviour was the predominant focus. Here it is God and the covenant relationship God has established with me. That relationship is such that God's love is offered to me unconditionally, and as grace. I enter into this relationship through faith, and in this encounter experience salvation and liberation as pure gift. It is my acceptance of God's acceptance of me that becomes the challenge of my faith, my life and my religion. Faith here is not so much a communication of facts about God as it is an experience of God's self-communication. As St John of the Cross reminded us, "Faith ... communicates God Himself to us" [C.12.4].

In Model A, my security came very much from my performance; here it comes from the realisation of God's unconditional love. Here I am okay, not because of my achievements but because of God's acceptance and love. Such an attitude is central to the Christian notion of humility which allows me to experience my worthlessness and my worth both at the same time, my worthlessness alone, and my worth in and through Christ. This experience of unconditional love moves me and empowers me to respond by loving others as I have been loved. 'Love one another as I have loved you' becomes the motivational key for my behaviour. My motivation is love, or pastoral charity, which flows predominantly from my experience of being loved [John 15:12]. At first sight, this model of spirituality can look like something of a sop, a cop out. As one approaches it from a distance, it can feel like an entry into licentiousness. [1 Peter 2:16; Galatians 5:13] In reality, it is much more demanding than the performance model described earlier.

For me to accept the unconditional love of God and respond accordingly is a most difficult challenge; it is completely disarming and all-embracing. It places my security and peace outside of my control and makes me dependent on another for my life and everything it implies. Love is only easy for those who do not know its power. Nevertheless, it is a sweet yoke and in the end a light burden. [Matthew: 11:30]. When I reflect on the agony and ecstasy of love, I cannot but recall my favorite Philippians text [Philippians 3:5-11] and its hint that, in some mysterious way, dying and rising, sacrifice and resurrection go together.

Evaluation

On the positive side

- Where previously the focus was on fear or a sort of cold justice, here it is on unconditional love. God loves me no matter what. Indeed, there is a sense in which the needier I am the more he is there for me! [Matthew 18:12; Mark 2:17; Romans 5:18].

- The centre of attention in this model is clearly God, not myself. I'm okay only because God accepts me. The image of God here is the one given in revelation. Here is a personal God who is the Father of Jesus; the one without whom I can do nothing (John 3:27). Whenever I succeed, all I can rightly do is give thanks. In this sense, it embodies a eucharistic spirituality. I believe it was Friedrich Schleiermacher who somewhere spoke of religion as an experience of ultimate dependence, not a matter of metaphysics or morality.

- My security in this model comes not from my success but as a gift of God's unconditional love. 'Peace is my gift to you' (John 14:27). This is the Good News for the poor in spirit and the humble. As already noted, true humility allows me to hold my brokenness and limitation in tension with my dignity as a child of God.

- In this model, one can own the fact that one is poor spiritually and indeed a sinner, yet nevertheless loved by God. I am not tempted to trim down the demands of the Gospel to fit my capabilities. I'm reminded of the statement of the Jesuits that insists that to be a Jesuit is to know that one is a sinner, yet called to be a companion of Jesus as Ignatius was. Here one is able to live with questions and pursue that degree of truth and goodness that lie beyond our present grasp. I can accept the proposition of being both saint and sinner at the same time. Daily conversion is an ongoing challenge and a blessing.

- Here, the quality of mercy, which is God's fullest reality, is uppermost in our experience of God. From this experience, one is motivated and empowered to be merciful, compassionate and forgiving to others. Here the awareness of our failings encourages us to turn even more to God who invites the troubled to lay their cares on God for forgiveness and healing. [Matthew 11:28-30] The more I fail, the more I need to go to God, whereas in the earlier model my failings put a barrier between God and myself.

- The motive for change is not that I might become more acceptable to myself or to God but that I might accept the self-gift of God more fully for my own greater life and the lives of those I walk and share with. Because God is personal and in relationship with us, God is close enough to be experienced, and we can dialogue with God and be guided by God speaking through the Spirit within. Here, we begin to understand that law in our hearts referred to in Jeremiah 31:33.

On the negative side

- In many ways, there is a feeling of less certitude in this model. The knowing here is a faith knowledge whereas in the other model the way of knowing God and God's ways may be little more than an exercise in rationalism based on some always fallible philosophical system or other. Model A can so easily revert to a rational type of knowing wherein the secrets are possessed not by the little ones but by the wise and learned [Matthew 11:25]. John of the Cross contrasts the knowledge of faith and that of reason noting that faith brings certitude to the intellect [but] does not produce clarity. [A2. 62.]

- The knowledge here is more intuitive and engages various faculties together: rational, affective, behavioural, social and spiritual. The science of religious experience distinguishes two forms of knowledge, referring to one as experimental [where one can be reflectively aware of one's knowing] and experiential [where, when one turns to reflect, the experience as such is no longer there]. It is not readily available to reflective consciousness. It demands levels of trust and the daring to walk on the words of our faith. Again John of the Cross helps with his statement that the journey of faith is the willingness to relinquish control: "As regards this road to union, entering on the road means leaving one's own road". A.2.4.5 In this model, the path to follow is less clear, less familiar and less open to be controlled. In this model, conscience is central to the living of life; and discernment is the way to the will of God. Truth becomes personal and is found not in the cleverest of arguments by the wise and learned but in relationship [John

14/16]. The understanding of and initiation into conscience formation and discernment processes are vital for those entering the unitive way and are probably incomprehensible for those who remain in the two earlier ways. A little more will be said on this critical issue later on. However, it is a matter requiring detailed and expert attention in our contemporary Church where too often we detect amongst leaders the trauma of the blind leading the blind. Conscience is a topic waiting to be explored in our formation of the masses [Matthew 15:14].

- As the years pass, I become more convinced that my own greatest temptation comes from my need to control my life in all of its many aspects. Indeed, I am indebted to an old friend Bernie Parker OCSO who, one day while I was on retreat at Tarrawarra Abbey, brought me to meditate on the trees in the Garden of Eden. There I saw how in my life I had been focused primarily on the tree of the knowledge of good and evil and basically neglecting the tree of life [Genesis 3:3].

- This Model B is not so easy to talk about in precise terms and its reality involves paradox. It is shared more through poetry, parables, images, in dialogue and through symbols. It is hard to tell anyone about it without first connecting with them and loving them with a passion. In the earlier model, it was critical to get things right because the 'things' had become godlike. Here things can afford to be more chaotic and messy. We can be at home with a God who chooses to be born in a manger [Luke 2:7].

- This is clearly a relational model and hard to come to and live by without some real experiences of human love, acceptance and forgiveness. These qualities one would hope to find mediated through one's presbyterate and/or local Church community, called as they are to be seedbeds of holiness. Too often they are not; and priests who have moved through to this

kind of spirituality typically identify things like involvement with Charismatic Renewal, a directed retreat, ongoing spiritual direction, falling in love and such like experiences of intimacy as the gates through which they passed.
- This is the spirituality of a God who always blesses before sending out, a God who always says 'Come' before saying 'Go'. To the extent that it puts the issue of love in the context of first being loved, it is truly biblical. Obviously, rules and creeds are still important but they are not central or crippling. As I understand it, this is the kind of spirituality that goes with the evangelisation we are hoping for as we approach the third millennium.

Caution

In many ways, these two spiritualties that I have described as representing opposite poles on a mythical continuum might be seen as parodies. In reality, it would be hard to find either one in pure form - after all they are models! All of us would be somewhere between the two extremes, with one or other model predominating. Hopefully, there would be a living fluidity, moving us ever onwards. A nice image would see us as truly a pilgrim people 'under canvas and on the road', not settled, not stagnant nor in fixed dwellings.

Converting from Model A Spirituality to Model B

Again the phenomenon of conversion, dying and rising, comes into its own and here the move is a big one as we seek to enter the unitive way! In this second call I see myself being moved across the desert that takes me from a Model A spirituality to Life in the Spirit according to Model B. While recalling that I am talking about experiences that go beyond words and ultimately defy definition, phrases like 'a move from religion to spirituality', 'from ethics or ideology to faith', 'from legalism to Christianity', a call to 'baptism in the Spirit', all have an enlightening quality to them.

For me, the Dark Night of the Soul is a powerful term for describing the experience of being moved over from what has been described as the Illuminative to the Unitive Way. Indeed, the feeling can be like that of losing one's soul, or in the words of the *Man of La Mancha*, of 'marching into hell for a heavenly cause!' It was here that I began to see and accept the weeds in the fields of my life where I thought that only wheat was acceptable [Matthew 13:24-30]. I began to see the vice mixed in with my virtue, and conversely, the virtue in with my vices. For example, my efforts to conform to the pattern of the ideal priest were motivated a lot from fear of failure, self-respect and my need to be in control and to be thought well of. Then too in conforming to this idealistic pattern, I was exposing myself to an experience of a God who was much more demanding and less accepting than the God of Jesus.

Need I mention that it is not at all easy to have one's customary and integrated image of God challenged? From a life characterised by an attitude of either/or, where what matters is knowing the clear lines between what is right and wrong, and true and false, I moved to face the trauma of being a both/and person. To borrow the title words of John V. Taylor's award-winning book, the Spirit became "The Go- Between God", and with Simone Weil I came to appreciate that the pinpoint of truth is the place where opposites sit together. From being a God only of righteousness, justice, power and order, my God became more a God of gentleness, mercy and compassion. My great entree to God is not my success but my poverty, even my failure. All I can boast of is my weakness; it alone is my strength. My only true prayer is 'Lord, be merciful to me a sinner' [Luke 18:13]. Texts such as these constantly call me forth to new life!

In trying to map out the terrain of this part of the spiritual life, I'm reminded that it is the Way of the Cross and as such it is mystery par excellence. It is not a place or a journey that I can set myself to take, nor is it a journey that I can lead another into. All that I can hope to do is yield to the grace, if and when it comes, and accompany my friends when they are called to make it. For those who have tasted this conversion call as a Way of the Cross, reflecting on it as such can be a source of strength, for those who have not so experienced it, it may well be a scandal [1 Corinthians 1:18].

A LOST STORY

As I think about the Cross as both power and scandal, I wonder if it is this arcane, mysterious and even dangerous nature of the spiritual life that explains why, as seminarians, we were neither told nor warned about how it might go for us when we got out there on the track and under way. Perhaps it is true that there are certain things about the spiritual life that are best kept from the beginners or the uninitiated. Maybe this explains why our general catechesis has been general and un-nuanced, especially in the connected areas of spirituality and morality.

Whatever the explanation, it remains one of the Church's greatest failings that she has encouraged her sons and daughters to launch out on the spiritual pilgrimage without providing them with sufficient support or information as to what might occur or how to handle it. Truly, in letting this happen, even facilitating it, she has abused them. Addressing this failing is surely amongst the most important challenges facing us today where institutional structures and a systemic culture are without doubt formed by factors embedded in a Model A behaviour-based spirituality.

To stress the point again: Where I am heading in this presentation is to claim that the institutional processes of education and formation in our Church are frozen to immature stages of maturity that rely too much on fear, law and order and control which deprive too many of the experience of Christianity as Love.

In the area of conversion, there is a parallel between what happens to us as individuals and what happens to us in our groups and institutions. Conversion calls us as individuals and as groups, parishes and communities. Again, it is my firm belief that our institutions and systems are basically structures still firmly operating from a behaviour-based spirituality, yet they now find themselves challenged, in a life/death struggle, to come alive in a new world.

In terms of the distinction between behaviour-based and relationally-focused spiritualties, I can still be living from a behaviour-based spirituality even though I am employing phrases and concepts that make it sound like I have moved beyond there to live relationally. I can still be basically living my life with God as an ideology with its dogma and its ethic of laws even though my language had been renewed. Personally, I find that the journey from the ways of ideology to those of deeper spirituality has been truly taking me via the Dark Night of the Soul, that particular Way of the Cross.

It has been suggested that upwards of 70% of our Church leaders have a predominantly behaviourist/ideological style of spirituality. If this diagnosis is correct - and I suspect that essentially it is - then I see a blueprint for the way our renewal must go and the challenges involved in addressing what can easily become an abusive entity. With Pope Paul VI, I can see that the crisis today is a crisis of faith. With Pope John Paul II, I can see that the way ahead into the third millennium is evangelisation, understood as bringing people into relationship and ultimately a personal relationship with the Lord.

The extent to which the more developed stages of the spiritual journey can be put into institutional form is debatable. Maybe all that can be hoped for from the institutional structures is that they do not block the growth of individuals, and somehow find ways to point people in the right direction. For this to happen, leaders must be people who, in Henri Nouwen's phrase, have moved from the moral to the mystical. As he further explains in *In The Name Of Jesus* (New York, Crossroads, 1989): " ... for the future of Christian leadership it is of vital importance to reclaim the mystical aspect of theology so that every word spoken, every advice given, and every strategy developed can come from a heart that knows God intimately... Christian leaders cannot simply be persons who have well-informed opinions about the burning issues of our time. Their leadership must be rooted in the permanent, intimate relationship with the incarnate Word, Jesus, and they need to find there the source for their words, advice and guidance... Dealing with burning issues without being rooted in a deep personal relationship with God easily leads to divisiveness because, before we know it, our sense of self is caught up in our opinion about a given subject". Religious leaders without a deep personal relationship with God are likely to be abusive.

I want to make two final comments regarding the stages of spiritual growth.

Risk of loss

As already noted, as I approach the call to move from where I am to the next stage, the feeling on the inside can be that all that has been good is going to be lost. In moving from the Purgative to the Illuminative, the feeling can be one of moving from law and order to anarchy. In moving from the Illuminative to the Unitive, I can feel I am becoming irrational and losing control. Clearly, the words of the Gospel are inspired when they speak of being prepared to lose one's life in order to gain it, and of dying in order to live [John 12:25]. An experience of fellowship is important to support and sustain us in these journeys. That means more compassion than control, more spirit than structure.

Discovery of gain

While a sense of loss may be the felt experience and the risk as I approach the conversion points, it changes drastically once I have planted my feet firmly in the new land. Having 'passed over', the experience readily becomes one of having gained something wonderfully new while retaining all that was authentic in the previous stages. Truly, 'Every scribe who becomes a disciple in the kingdom of heaven is like a householder who brings out from his storeroom things both new and old' [Matthew 13:51-52].

Chapter Four

Concerning sexuality

The impact on sexuality of all that I am claiming here is such as to deserve a separate treatment all together. What follows is merely indicative rather than claiming to be adequate.

Maturity

It is generally accepted that sex and sexuality is for adults, and so requires a level of personal development that makes it possible for the participants to have ownership of their lives and an ability to allow others in. Short of that ability, 'sexual activity' cannot produce the kind of relationship and generativity that is its purpose. In the hands of the immature, it contracts from being a wondrous mystery to something with likely destructive consequences. How mature one's sexuality is will determine how one's relationships are and vice versa.

The simple claim that I offer is that the profiles of priests so far offered argue to a formation that makes true relationships and intimacy problematic and leaves one's sexuality unattended, underdeveloped and open to dysfunction. Thus the door is open for abuse; and in the context of 'the distortion of the greatest is the greatest distortion', the results can be and are catastrophic!

By way of unpacking such a claim, one needs to realise that as humans we are both individual and social/relational. What brings us into relationship is a drive of massive proportions, so great that Freud was able to describe it as 'the' basic instinct of the human personality. It might be repressed but it will not go away, and it will exercise its forces destructively until, hopefully, it will eventually challenge its user to a conversion inspired by the pain of its misuse. I stress this point from the belief that few, if any, of us get to integrate our sexuality without a struggle which puts us in touch with both the 'wheat and weeds' of what it is to be human. The struggle with sexuality can be a valuable pathway to integrity and wholeness; it can be a highway to experience God in God's highest form as Mercy. Hiding from sexuality with its passion, and acting as though it does not exist, is madness. Yet that can easily be a quality/feature of an immature Model A spirituality.

Our sexuality drives us towards relationships. I like the way Martin Buber speaks of one's ability to engage with another, be it a person or thing, as an "I" or as an "It". It is only in I-Thou engagements that connection is made and generativity achieved; and that is the mark of maturity.

Misunderstanding Sexuality

As a church, the problem we have with sexuality is due not only to the inability of our clerical leaders to engage in mature intimate relationships, it is due also to our corporate understanding of sexuality and our overall experience with it. It is important to recall that our faith experience has intellectual, emotional, behavioural and social components and that a movement in any one impacts on each of the others as well as on the whole. The image of the polyhedron used by Pope Francis in his address at the Independence Hall in Philadelphia [20 September 2015] and subsequent Apostolic Exhortation provides us with a precious tool with which to grasp the inter-dependence of these elements. The exclusively intellectual understanding we have had of sex moulds our experience of it and the consequent place it plays in our lives. This in turn feeds back to influence our intellectual understanding, and, because of the inherent confusion it would be hard to find any other element of human experience immersed in so many dysfunctional myths. Such myths stimulate specific behaviours and in turn mould future understandings.

Sex was thought about and discussed long before the dawn of Christianity, and the early church community adopted many of those earlier insights. Not only were the insights taken over. They in turn impacted on behavioral patterns and social forms within the developing Christian institution. Behaviours, beliefs and taboos that came from non-Christian sources were incorporated and integrated and even read back into Scripture. In 2005, the Humanita Foundation, along with the Australian Catholic University, commissioned three public lectures, to be given independently in different States by different scholars, entitled, *What the Bible says about Sex?*

Surprisingly, for many in the audience, the answer was "very little, if indeed anything at all"! That, of course, is the generally accepted position of biblical scholars worldwide but one that has not been readily disseminated, possibly because of the threat it poses to the belief systems of so many people and to so much that we have absorbed into our cultures. Much of the incredible detail that we do have concerning sex comes from social and/ or cultural sources, rather than from divine inspiration. The urgent need for a thorough revamp of our teachings on sex has been dramatically highlighted by many. One such was the late Jesuit Psychiatrist, Dr James J. Gill, who, when speaking of our understanding of sex and sexuality, said, "There were so many 'ignorances' and dysfunctional myths that need not exist and these were causing great pain and awful behaviour which was clearly a burden to the Church and its mission to evangelise". Genuine moral theologians, as distinct from the more canonically minded, have been aware of this for some time but they, along with their findings, have been vilified with an intensity hard to understand, such is the power base occupied by sex in our lives and the strength generated by an immature Model A type spirituality.

Systemic Change

Immerse immature individuals within this flawed environment and the dysfunctional outcome for many is assured. Amongst other things, I would claim as obvious that [i] the totality of our doctrinal and moral positions in general, but especially with regard to relationships, needs to be revisited and up-dated. I have every confidence that the scholarship and the technical means to achieve this are readily available. [ii] What is urgently needed is a "change of mind and heart" on behalf of those in positions of authority to author the new life that is needed. After all, that is what authority is; and the model for people in roles of authority is more one of a conductor of an orchestra than a general of an army. The problem, as I am proposing it, is primarily in the system and its administration; and the healing has to be in a reformed style of leadership. Of course, I am not advocating that all will or can be expected to move to the levels of consciousness or awareness appropriate to the higher levels of development; at least not in the immediate future. What I am advocating, however, is that our education/formation structures will be open to such developments, and that a sufficient percentage of our leaders will be at least cognisant of such advanced developments. The science of religious experience distinguishes these two forms of knowledge: referring to one as experimental, where one can be reflectively aware of one's knowing; and other experiential, where, when one turns to reflect, the experience is no longer there.

Shame and Control

Two very clear aspects of sexuality that have played a central part in the way it has become a part of our Catholic culture are the inherent ability of sexuality to give rise to shame and fear and its ability to be a source of power and control. The power of pleasure and its ability to take over one's life has threatened and frightened men [mainly men!] from time immemorial. Anything that might overpower us was seen as a threat, and controlling that threat was a goal for any rounded human being. Getting on top of one's irrational drives was admirable, and philosophers set out to find ways and means to do this. Sex, of course, was one of the obvious contenders, as were eating and drinking.

Inconsistency

The different ways in which these pleasures were treated is interesting. With food, it was the excess indulgence in the pleasure of eating that became the point of attention, not the food as such. With sex, of course, it was the act, the very source of the pleasure, that found its way into the world of prohibition. The cure for the threat from food was found in discipline and temperance etc., and not really in designating any food itself a "forbidden fruit". There is a wisdom here that needs to be revived. It would appear that the early Greeks were not so much concerned with what one did or did not do, but rather with the effects or consequences of one's action.

It is because of the similarity between eating and sex that comparisons have been made with questions such as, "What if we were to treat eating in the same way as we treat sex?" Some would argue that, if we were to be consistent, then we would have to ban Cook Books because their main aim would seem to be to enhance the pleasure we gain in eating. Chewing-gum would be certainly banned as it has no nutritional value and only stimulates the senses of the mouth. Owning restaurants and being chefs would be dubious professions - and so we might go on. The objectivising of the action to discredit sex as such is significant and fits in easily with the "way" of life appropriate to the earlier stages of moral and spiritual development. At a later date, when St Augustine came to link sex with the invasive phenomenon of "original sin", a tectonic shift came to our already negative appreciation of sex that has continued even to this very day. From here, the move to dissect sexual actions into various categories [and even pre-action thoughts and desires] easily followed.

Misusing Fear

Amidst such developments, life itself became a thing to fear; and the Church, looking for ways to exercise 'helpful' power and control over its members, saw the power that could be gained if only she could control sex. Over-idealised standards were demanded, and the institution, through the sacrament of penance, became the only source of relief. The linking of sex and sin came to be an amazing tool for control and was pursued into our own era despite the incredible distortions and damage it has done to the health of the Church's membership.

Sex, fear and shame can be powerful partners and seek out darkness and secrecy. Like the tentacles of a mythical beast, they penetrate into every cranny and corner of our life. With differing focuses at different times of the journey, they provide a major, if not the major, challenge to a community set on health and renewal.

It is claimed, and probably correctly, that the incidence of abuse within the Church has abated. This in itself is no argument that the real problem has been addressed. The current reaction and approach of governing bodies that engender fear, along with the increasing dynamics of control, would be enough to explain the downturn of occurrences. But that, of course, is not the Christian way to health and holiness!

Sex is the power that moves us physically, psychologically, socially, and spiritually and who knows in what other ways to *connect creatively*. If we are not connecting in ways that are healthy, creative and generative, then we are going to be in trouble. This is especially true for those of us who are trying to live celibately. If we are being governed by controlling authorities whose main aim is to protect the system and who try to 'lead' without dialogue and true communication, then we are truly being abused and our needs to be expressive and creative are stifled. In the bygone world of Christendom, clergy were given a form of social connectedness and had a generative part to play in and through building their communities with bricks and mortar as well as other tangible ways. In those days, the temptations to misuse our sexual faculties were screened to a great extent by the social taboos and inherent fears within the immature stages of moral development that were being promulgated. Today such "helps" have disappeared. We clergy are readily taken for granted, told what to do, inhibited by the need for senseless permissions – and bombarded by sexual stimulation to a degree unimagined before. Where are the structures to support us in such an idealistic vocation?

Chapter Five

The issue of leadership

Of particular interest to this presentation is the question of power and authority and the use thereof. Given the stilted formation processes within our ecclesiastical institutions, I am proposing that both our priests and laity are too often being led in dysfunctional and abusive ways.

In order to establish a context, may I begin by quoting from *The Harvard Address* of Alexander Solzhenitsyn delivered in 1978. In quoting from this document, I also note my belief that the problems I am hoping to highlight in the Church are not confined to that particular institution but are endemic in all the basic structures of our western world. While this fact can provide us with some relief, it also highlights the challenge upon us to serve our world with the Good News of the Gospel in the admirable spirit of *Gaudium et Spes* [para 1].

Solzhenitsyn says:

"Western society has given itself the organisation best suited to its purposes, based I would say, on the letter of the law... Any conflict is solved according to the letter of the law and this is considered to be the supreme solution. If one is right from a legal point of view, nothing more is required, nobody may mention that one could still not be entirely right, and urge self-restraint, a willingness to renounce such legal rights, sacrifice and selfless risk: it would sound simply absurd. One almost never sees voluntary self-restraint. Everybody operates at the extreme limit of those legal frames. An oil company is legally blameless when it purchases an invention of a new type of energy in order to prevent its use... I have spent all my life under a communist regime and I will tell you that a society without any objective legal scale is a terrible one indeed. But a society with no other scale but the legal one is not quite worthy of man either. A society, which is based on the letter of the law and never reaches any higher, is taking very scarce advantage of the high level of human possibilities. The letter of the law is too cold and formal to have a beneficial influence on society. Whenever the tissue of life is woven of legalistic relations there is an atmosphere of moral mediocrity, paralyzing man's noblest impulses. And it will be simply impossible to stand through the trials of this threatening century with only the support of a legalistic structure". [The editing within the text is mine.]

Obviously, as an organisation, the Church needs to initiate her members into certain modes of behaviour, attitudes, ways of thinking, etc. Unless this type of thing is done, no organisation or institution can function. This process of education and moral formation is necessary for the life of the Church.

Power

Those who are in charge of this socialising process are in a position of power. "Power is an actor's ability to induce or influence another actor to carry out his directions or any other norms he supports" [Etzioni, A. (1978). Comparative analysis of complex organizations. In D. Hampton, C. Summer, & R. Weber (eds), *Organizational behavior and the practice of management*. Glenview, IL: Scott Foresman & Co.]. The dilemma comes when we realise that there is a use of power that is consistent with the Gospel and a use of power that is inimical to it.

The problem involved in the use of power is the danger that it might be used to 'overpower' rather than to 'empower'. Overpowering belongs to servitude, to using force, fear, etc.; and clearly the Gospel is not about that. Overpowering gives rise to passivity, anger, resentment, and a lack of empathy for those who are in the positions of power or authority. It is not the outcome produced by one who claims to be a disciple of Jesus who said,

"All this I tell you that my joy may be yours and your joy may be complete. This is my commandment: love one another as I have loved you. I no longer speak of you as slaves for a slave does not know what his master is about. Instead I call you friends since I have made known to you all that I heard from my Father" [John 15:11-15].

"I came that they might have life and have it to the full ... I am the good shepherd, I know my sheep and my sheep know me, in the same way that the Father knows me and I know the Father" [John 10:10-15].

The type of influence or causality envisioned in the Gospel between the actions of the leader and the actions of the led is not an efficient causality that belongs to the world of objects, but a final causality that belongs to the world of persons. I recall well words from a lecture by Sister Evelyn Woodward, "It is 'relational' not 'unilateral' power!"

'Unilateral' power

We must remember that behaviour-based spirituality [Model A], embracing states that I have chosen to gather under the imagery of the Purgative and the Illuminative stages of the faith journey, involves an objective type of worldview and gravitates to notions of efficient causality – as we well know from the way that the theology of grace and sacramental theology have developed under the influence of that model. As one critic was heard to say, "Grace could be dispensed by the bucket load!"

It is my belief that, in the area of ethics or moral theology, the 'subjective' succumbed to the 'objective' and practically everything came to be handled within the discipline of law.

I recall how those who taught Moral Theology during my seminary years were in the most part trained in the discipline of Canon Law. I readily recall the story of a prominent priest who was called in by the vicar general of one of our metropolitan archdioceses and informed that he had been nominated for postgraduate studies in Rome. When he asked what sort of studies, he was told that he could decide and so went off to think and pray. When he returned to declare that his choice was to study dogmatic theology, he was informed that it would need to be something practical and so was sent off to study Canon Law. [That man died only recently.]

In secular institutions, more often than not, the main concern is that the desired behaviour is produced, while the reasons why the subject conforms are of secondary consideration. The institutionalised model is concerned almost exclusively with a consideration of externals or visibles. In his book titled *Life In Abundance – A Contemporary Spirituality* (Mahwah, NJ, Paulist Press, 1983), Francis Baur provides some helpful material by tracing this objectifying tendency back to our philosophical roots and noting that the God of the philosopher, the un-moved mover, the supreme being, the infinite one , etc. is not the God of scripture. He goes on to note that the institutional life-style creates its own theology; and comments further; "We are persons not objects, and we are more true to our essential selfhood when we respond from the wealth of our own power of choice, rather than when power is imposed upon us. We feel most abused and demeaned when the will of another is imposed upon our own, when threat or force of whatever sort – psychological, emotional, physical – supplies the coercion which causes our will to submit. In these cases, we do not choose straightforwardly the proffered good; we choose, rather the avoidance of evil to ourselves."

'Relational' power

When we consider the Church and its Gospel mission, the paradox of the Gospel is seen again in clear light. For the Gospel, the external is secondary; the important element is the inner spirit. Jesus stood out against, and indeed suffered because of, the stance he took against the legalism of his day. He placed the source of behavior in the heart, in the deepest recesses of the person. The power to act in a Christian sense must come from within; the values and norms that belong to the society must be internalised if they are to be embraced and work in human beings in a human way. What I am implying here is that conscience - the voice of the Spirit within - is supreme, and that faith, not mere obedience, is the Christian response. It is a fundamental tenet of our tradition, but it needs to be stressed very much in our contemporary environment.

"I will place my law within them, and write it upon their hearts. I will be their God and they shall be my people. No longer will they have need to teach their friends and kinsmen how to know the Lord" [Jeremiah [31:33-34].

"You Pharisees! You cleanse the outside of cup and dish, but within you are filled with rapaciousness and evil. Fools! Did not he who made the outside make the inside too" [Luke 11:39-40].

Conformity

What can be easily lost in bringing about conformity is the inner conviction and agreement which lead to actions that flow from the heart, and therefore cheerfully and with freedom. If actions do not so flow, then the actor must understandably feel used and manipulated; he or she may repress that feeling for one or another reason; nevertheless, it can still operate and poison the spirit of the person. To achieve conformity at the cost of this inner spring is to have achieved nothing - from a Christian point of view - for the person so acting. To conform, in itself, is not Christian. If I find myself committed to a set of ideas, convinced that these have to be imposed on myself and others, then I may be moved by a powerful ideology but not by Christian faith.

The tension involved is not an easy one, and the temptation to resolve it by way of overpowering is ever present and strong. Jesus experienced such temptations, and they stand in the Gospel to warn us and strengthen us. [Matthew 4:1-11]

It must be stressed that in all these considerations we are dealing with adult Christians. Many times, excuses for violating conscience are proposed on the grounds that the people in question need clear guidelines - perhaps what is behind such statements is that they need to be told what to do. It may well be that this is true. Whenever we do treat adults in this way, let us realise that we are treating them as children and confirming them in their immaturity. We must never justify this violation of conscience as a virtue! It is such an exercise of authority that disempowers and retards many priests.

Let me digress for a moment. In order to rest my mind and re-focus, I have just gone to my music file and played a video rendition of Strauss's *Blue Danube waltz* with orchestra, conductor and a ballet background. I could not but feel that so much of all that I am struggling to express here was being played out there before me: the formation in the various disciplines as background for the inner creative spirits of the various artists, all of this being expressed under the baton of the conductor. The ultimate essence of authority was there before my eyes, to draw forth the story, the spirit within, not to impose a story from without – each player, each dancer, was contributing to the ultimate masterpiece.

Priesthood impoverished

Father Paul Keys has an interesting autobiographical story that merits repetition: "As one successful old pastor put it to me when I was first ordained; 'Father, you must understand that the Church is not a playground. It is more like an army. I am the general and you young curates are my lieutenants. We can't allow confusion, disrespect, or subversion among the troops. Learn to keep a safe distance from the people. They don't know where they are going and so we must be ready at all times to tell them what is allowed and what isn't. It takes courage to be a strong leader like this'. Fortunately, I smiled and left his parish 'headquarters' and, I hope, went out to minister to God's people as a servant."

What we do, our behaviour, can become an important issue, and in fact it has too often become the important issue. None of us should accept that what we do, or do not do, is our central concern; such an idea is clearly abhorrent. However, the evidence is there to show that this is the way we have been encouraged to behave within our Church formation structures. One has only to remember the 'experience of sin' that belonged to our confessional practice of recent times to see the evidence. If I missed Mass, I committed a sin; the intention or freedom that I possessed during such an external event was in fact of secondary consideration. One might claim a more egregious example in citing the way that sexual thoughts and desires came to be treated: such subjective material became objectified and seen as sin as soon as they arose. Another interesting example may be found in the way we separated the internal and the external forum in seminary days. Certainly, if you could find ways not to get caught, you were assured of making it to ordination! Too many who were responsible for formation were obedient and conforming men unable to engage with the subjective realities of those in their care.

The profiles of priests referred to earlier highlight the fact that we have been concerned minimally with the spirit and in this we have gone the way of the world around us, which is drained of spirit – as Solzhenitsyn pointed out as the main point of his famous Harvard address quoted at the beginning of this chapter. To give this 'spirit' back to our world is surely our mission; how important is it then that we find it in our own midst and quickly?

In the concern that we have had for others and also in the concern that others have had for us, the external became all-important. Consequently, we manipulated and were manipulated to conform for their/our own good and the salvation of their/our souls. The intention, perhaps, was admirable. The process, diabolical!

Priesthood renewed

It is evident from the recent documentation coming from the Magisterium that all stops are out to reverse any aberrations in the use of power. Freedom of conscience statements, Priest Councils, the rights of the laity, consultation, joy in gospel living etc. are just a few examples that quickly come to mind. Be that as it is, the new models will not survive unless we put them into new wineskins. What the Council warned us is true. We are not just being given new ideas or gimmicks: we are being called to *metanoia*, which is a change of mind and heart. This is much more than new ideas, skills, etc. It demands a whole change of values.

As far as we priests are concerned, there is another Catch 22 involved with this question of power. Sure, we suffer under it but we also can use it to give us a sense of importance and status. On one hand we suffer under it, while on the other hand we benefit from it and have a precious place for it in our world-view or spirituality. How often do we cry about wanting them – whoever they might be – to change? Maybe the one who first needs to change is the one sitting in our chair!

Sense of Joy

We are all familiar with St Paul's exhortation to the Corinthians concerning 'generous giving': "Each one should give what they have decided in their own mind, not grudgingly or because they are made to, for God loves a cheerful giver" [2 Corinthians 9:7].

Clearly, that quotation was made in the context of a special collection. However, its application to any act of giving seems to be valid, and it has constantly been used in a wider context. The principles are important: giving according to an interior decision, not grudgingly, or because we are somehow forced into it, and giving cheerfully. Its message joins in with that other important statement of the New Testament: "Come to me all you who are weary and find life burdensome, and I will refresh you. Take my yoke upon your shoulders and learn of me, for I am gentle and humble of heart. Your souls will find rest, for my yoke is easy and my burden light." [Matthew 11:28-30].

From the profiles of priests, it is clear that there is a lack of cheerfulness and joy in our giving. There is evidence of 'drivenness' and joylessness, an extreme anxiety that denies peace. This is disturbing, and allows us to take seriously the statement of Frs Thomas Kane and Paul Keys who write in the context of the American diocesan priest: "If the modern American parish priest is guilty of anything, it might be that he has often tried too hard." And they go on to say that we are invited to live 'reflectively' not 'reactively' [as so many men in diocesan ministry do].

Pope Paul VI in his *Apostolic Exhortation* of 9 May 1975, along with Francis in his recent Encyclical *Evangelii Gaudium*, proclaim this same message of joy in their call to interior renewal and reconciliation in Christ.

For many of us, these words are a challenge and indeed even something of a condemnation of our 'lifestyle' or spirituality. This joy in the Lord and the freedom of God's children are not all that obvious!

"If the son frees you, you will really be free" [John: 8:36].

"Give thanks to God the Father always and for everything in the name of Our Lord Jesus Christ" [Ephesians 5:20].

"Christ's peace must reign in your hearts, since as members of the one body you have been called to that peace. Dedicate yourselves to thankfulness. Let the word of Christ, rich as it is, dwell in you. Sing gratefully to God from your hearts in psalms, hymns, and inspired songs" [Colossians:3:15-17].

In presenting the two models of spirituality outlined above, we have tried to indicate that these gospel qualities and their absence in our lives are very much factors of the level of our spirituality and to the way we have put our lives together.

Chapter Six

Making moral choices

How might we begin to understand what is going on?

When we consider the Church and its Gospel mission, then the paradox of the Gospel is seen again in clear light. For the Gospel, the external is secondary; the important element is the heart. The Beatitudes are 'be-attitudes', and call for being as the basis for doing. The institutionalised model is built up almost exclusively from a consideration of externals or visibles, and is prone to a legalistic approach.

Guilt And The Superego

Superego

Related to this concentration on externals and the consequent bypassing of the Spirit is the way in which we are socialised and the way we socialise. At the risk of repeating myself, there are many ways of getting people to conform. You can 'force' them from outside or from inside.

The forcing from within by means of engaging shame and inappropriate guilt feelings is something that we as Church have made use of, and it contributes in no small way to some of our current problems. Relevant to our concerns is the psychological reality known as the superego which gives rise to *feelings of guilt*. It operates mainly below the threshold of consciousness and isolates our drives and impulses from rational control. Therefore, it operates irrationally.

One of the best treatments of the superego that I know, and one that is borrowed in current books on moral theology and conscience, is that of John Glaser, S .J. [*Theological Studies.* Vol. 32. No: 4. Dec 1971. Pp. 30-47]. Because of the unquestionable relevance of this material, I would encourage you, the reader, to source that article as an authoritative critique of my following presentation.

You will recall how earlier on I referred to the dynamic where the Church was able to handle the behavioural issues of her members by implanting within them a kind of moral policeman who acted from within and monitored their behaviour. That earlier understanding of mine served me well and led me to an appreciation of the various spirits which can prompt us in our lives. It also directed me back into the tradition where the existence of different spirits, good and bad, and the importance of recognising the one from the other, was of supreme importance. The word used to identify this ability to recognise the good from the bad was *discernment*, and it referred to realities far more sophisticated than those referred to as discernment today. Regularly, one will hear of individuals or groups 'discerning' some decision when nothing has taken place other than a decision has been made by one or more within the interested group, often the more powerful amongst them.

According to the analysis of human development and the status of spirituality that I have proposed as behavioural-based Model A, discernment and true conscience belong to a level of maturity and development that is beyond the majority within the Church community! In the earlier stages of moral trainings, in contrast to moral education, we see the internalising of the voice of an authority figure and the coercing of the subject to conform. How such a dynamic can involve abuse of an individual should be clear.

However, before I get ahead of myself, let me return to my story of the good and the evil spirits; and let me say how my earlier understanding was enriched when I was eventually introduced to Sigmund Freud and his exposition on the super-ego. Subsequent to Freud, modifications have been made to his presentation, but basically his initial insights, which are of prime interest to us, remain valid.

Challenges

Need I say it again that most of our moral catechesis in the recent past, and our collapsed confessional practice built upon it, have been subverted by such a superego approach. Understandably, when modern education began to spread amongst the masses, a revolt occurred, challenging the Church to rediscover and teach anew the grace that is conscience. The obvious need for an intelligent and modern exposé on conscience for the masses can and must be provided by others more competent than I am. My purpose is simply to highlight the need for such an exposé and to point out the damage being spread while we retain a superego morality built on fear and an exaggerated sense of authority.

Of particular interest is the current practice for electing leaders, in particular, bishops. The pledge of allegiance required of possible candidates ensures the likelihood that Model A men will be chosen, and a system already haemorrhaging at the edges will be retained. Such is the challenge facing an institution in moving from an inappropriate moral base to a base in the spirit. In the words of the late great Cardinal of Milan, Carlo Martini, supported also by Karl Rahner, we are challenged to move from being a Church of morals to become a mystic Church.

Often, I have been misunderstood, opposed and even attacked by fellow Church members when I have tried to introduce this nuanced understanding. Of course, the conversion required and the trauma involved in transversing the "dark night" between one stage of spiritual experience to the next can be challenging, especially for those who have invested heavily into their accepted ways. [My own lack of sensitivity and tact, coming from my own immaturity, hurt and impatience, would also need to be calculated in assessing the slings and arrows that were fired.]

My appreciation, and indeed my understanding, of superego is greatly influenced by understanding of the treatment of spirits and our need to discern between them, as proclaimed and taught by the tradition. I have suggested above that we internalise the voices of authority figures and their demands in order to be accepted by them and be 'at one' with or loved by them. Once internalised, these voices take their place mainly in the subconscious, and are activated from there to exercise their power to modify or oppose any behaviour that is contrary to the original condemnation or disapproval. It works mainly as a subconscious voice. It can initiate good actions – for example, it can urge a child to refrain from putting a needle into a power point. But it can also echo voices inappropriate to another situation, voices which are in fact harmful – for example, it can reproach someone for missing Mass when at home in bed sick!

False guilt

My understanding is that when it is in any way in discord with the life-spirit which pulses in all situations and from which arises the voice of conscience, a dissonance or trauma of some kind results. The trauma or dissonance which I describe here is caused by a fear or false guilt and can be quite traumatic. Threatening one with the fear of loss of love, acceptance and approval is the equivalent to threatening one's life. The fury of a violated superego is immense, and is the greatest inhumanity one can rain on one's self. Freud has remarked that being loved is equivalent to life itself for the ego; and in my time I have seen it destroy bodies as well as souls. Man's inhumanity to man is equalled only to/by man's inhumanity to self which, more often than recognised, is the source of similar violence to others.

As I am describing them, there are two moral worlds existing in the normal person, a destructive force and a creative, life-giving one.

People under the control of superego can rightly be described as neurotic – and much of the behaviour generated by superego-imprisoned leaders gives birth to many of the so-called 'Catholic guilt' neuroses. People who have been the object of moral training rather than moral education will encounter particular difficulty in life. Of course, it is my contention that much of the formation process within our educational institutions relies on the superego rather than on the development of healthy conscience. One thing should be made very clear: and that is that the commands of the superego do not arise from any perception of the intrinsic goodness or objectionableness of the contemplated action. The inhumanity exercised within an individual by this Frankenstein of a reality is equal to any inhumanity exercised between persons in the outer world, and may well be an explanation of man's inhumanity to neighbour.

What Glaser has to say about what can reside within us as a tyrannical and "false conscience" is one of the most important keys to understanding the problem in priesthood today. Of course, it is my contention that 'Model A spirituality' people are much more prone to be under the influence of superego than of conscience.

Differentiating Superego and Genuine Conscience

Glaser draws up some interesting characteristic contrasts which exist between superego and genuine conscience.

SUPEREGO	CONSCIENCE
Commands that an act be performed for approval, in order to make oneself loveable, accepted; fear of love-withdrawal is the basis	Invites to action, to love, and in this act of other-directed commitment invites to co-create self-value
Introverted: the thematic centre is the sense of one's own value	Extroverted: the thematic centre is value which invites; self-value is concomitant and secondary to this
Static: does not grow, does not learn; cannot function creatively in a new situation; merely repeats a basic command	Dynamic: an awareness and sensitivity to value which develops and grows; a mindset with can precisely function in a new situation
Authority-figure-oriented: not a question of perceiving and responding to a value but of "obeying" authority's command "blindly"	Value-orientated: the value or disvalue is perceived and responded to, regardless of whether authority has commanded or not
"atomised" units of activity are its object	Individual acts are seen in their importance as a part of a larger process or pattern

Past-oriented: primarily concerned with cleaning up the record with regard to past acts	Future-oriented: creative; sees the past as having a future and helping to structure this future as a better future
Urge to be punished and thereby earn reconciliation	Sees the need to repair by structuring the future orientation toward the value in question (which includes making good past harms)
Rapid transition from severe isolation, guilt feelings, etc., to a sense of self-value accomplished by confessing to an authority figure	A sense of the gradual process of growth which characterises all dimensions of genuine personal development
Possible great disproportion between guilt experienced and the value in question; extent of guilt depends more on weight of authority figure and "volume" with which he speaks rather than density of the value in question	Experience of guilt proportionate to the importance of the value in question, even though authority many never have addressed this specific value

Glaser comments: "In light of this less than exhaustive list of contrasts, it should be clear that failing to distinguish these two realities will cause considerable confusion... The pastoral and ascetic practice which flows from such a superego-weighted interpretation of guilt, etc., will be to a great extent in conflict with man's genuine freedom".

Recall briefly that it is the contention of this work that it is the misguided or mistaken use of factors such as the superego, as a means of socialising priests and others into the patterns of behaviour deemed appropriate, that has been one of the significant causes of the profiles that we have identified. We have been caught up in the web of a foreign or evil spirit. To describe the superego as an evil spirit is no exaggeration at all.

Problems arising from confusion

Glaser goes on to reflect on some areas where it seems to him that we have been mistaken both in drawing theological conclusions and in projecting conduct (pastoral, ascetic, or sacramental) from data of the superego. In other words, he is about to describe aspects of our life that have been put together influenced by the superego. Let Glaser spell out some of the places where he sees that this unwise use of the superego has caused problems.

He begins his observations by saying: "All the following reflections could be subsumed under one rubric: too much theory and practice in the Church arises from data whose source is the superego. Many problem areas which have emerged in the recent past can be traced to a failure to recognise the nature, presence, and power of the superego" [p. 39]. I will try to summarise his main points.

God's Will – Human Will

Unless we distinguish superego from conscience (which we have not done adequately), we can quite easily confuse the voice of superego with the voice of God.

The spiritual masters were concerned precisely with this possibility when they focused on the need to know our inner selves and to practise the indispensable spiritual exercise of discernment of spirits. What is coming from the true spirit, what from the evil spirit? This discernment must be done in the presence of all 'seeming' goods; and under the heading of the evil spirit, they would include what we are calling superego.

In the document *Spiritual Renewal of the American Priesthood*, published by the United States Conference of Catholic Bishops in 1973, three dynamics are nominated as crucial for the priesthood today. They are:

- The ability to discern.
- The discernment of where the Death of Christ and the Resurrection of Christ are acting in our life.
- The interrelationship between contemplation and action.

In day-to-day living in the Church, many of our decisions are taken on purely human grounds! We make use of human reason, common sense, lobbying, consensus, etc. – all of which are very valid and useful human devices. In using these means, we will come to wise human decisions but always we must remember: 'My thoughts are not your thoughts, nor are my ways your ways', says the Lord. 'As high as the heavens are above the earth, so high are my ways above your ways, and my thoughts above your thoughts' [Isaiah 55:8-9. Also Wisdom 9:6.].

Once we have gathered all with the work of human hands, there is another step; and that step is so often not taken. Into the vacuum that our lack of discernment provides, there is a space for the superego to come in; and obviously it does, and even our human wisdom – which is different from true Wisdom – is polluted!

As is customary, myths were introduced to support the use of the superego as a power for socialising. Not only did we leave a vacuum for the superego to enter, we actually programmed the entry. We made statements like: "God will not be pleased with you if you do not do this or that", "The voice of the superior is the will of God" or "The fear of God is the beginning of wisdom". Maybe it is, but we were content to stay at the beginning and act as if the beginning was the entire reality!

Such statements as the myths noted above are interesting statements and, like all heresy, they contain an element of truth. Nevertheless, they are heretical all the same. Glaser writes: "To associate the mystery of invitation, the absolute yes to man's future, the radical call to eternally abiding love – God – with the hot and cold, arbitrary tyrant of the superego is a matter of grave distortion. [Superego] reaches into the totality of a person's explicitly religious life and poisons every fresh spring of the good news. Such a God deserves to die" [p. 39].

Whatever we might be saying on our lips, as long as we operate with superego to overpower people into whatever kind of behaviour, the experience that we have of God will be as of a tyrant or a demanding master, not the God of Jesus.

Concept of Sin and Guilt

As has already been noted, our whole theology of sin has become distorted because we have failed to recognise various kinds of guilt experience. "The nature of superego guilt and its radical difference from genuine moral guilt went unrecognised" [p. 40].

Glaser singles out for special comment the area of sexuality – which is notoriously susceptible to the tyranny of superego. Superego feelings of guilt in the matter of sexuality will obviously distort our whole handling of sexuality and cause untold problems. Along with this, it will flow on into the whole area of affectivity and there spread its poison. This we have recognised earlier in stating - as problem areas in the lives of priests - sexuality, sexual relationships and affectivity in general.

Superego and Confessional Practice

Glaser touches on a reality that is at the heart of the contemporary malaise or fall-off in one of the most precious and fruitful sacraments of our liturgy, the sacrament of Reconciliation. This malaise or fall-off is common to priests and laity alike. He writes: "It is, as traditionally realised, predominantly, though not exclusively, a service of the superego needs of individuals" [p. 42]. Maybe nowhere is the fact that we have used the superego in institutionalising more evident than in the way we distorted the celebration of this central sacrament. "This means that the phenomenon of diminishing confession is, at least in part, a healthy recognition of the misfit existing between genuine freedom and a system of categories – institutionalised in the traditional practice of confession – derived to a great extent from the superego. Therefore, this phenomenon (of non-use of the confessional), far from being regrettable, is a sign of health and insight" [p. 43].

After some reflection as to how the sacrament of Reconciliation might be restored, he goes on: "[new forms] ... demand that we recognise the reality of the superego for what it is and thereby avoid merely creating forms of serving the infantile needs of the superego in a new way" [p. 43].

If, as Glaser claims, the operation of superego has poisoned the celebration of reconciliation sacramentally, it can also be stated that the everyday exercise of reconciliation, so necessary for communal living, has also been poisoned by the side effects of immature [Model A] spirituality and superego. Maybe more than love, we need to rediscover forgiveness.

Superego and Blinding to Values

The superego distorts our image of God and our image of sin as we have already noted. It is a far more infallible tormentor of failure than a promoter of goodness. It is the perfect recipe for a poor self-image. It is powerful in setting up feelings of failure, frustration and depression! It sees the 'status quo' as sacrosanct in its disposition to merely repeat basic commands. By definition, it is static. It also leads us to selfish behaviour even if we put the most altruistic reasons forward for our actions. In this context, it is interesting to recall the very high percentage of priests in an American study who revealed that 'saving one's soul' was the most important thing in life. Superego is primarily concerned with the state of "soul" of the individual. Selfishness and self-centeredness is not at all uncommon in priests and religious. Rollo May's comment on "the divine right to be taken care of" amongst religious has already been noted.

Superego pulls us out of present orientations to an over concern with the past. Again this is a particular concern amongst priests; it can lead us to go through life looking over our shoulder. It can lead us to shirk responsibility by making 'blind obedience' into a virtue. Clearly, much of the resistance to valid and responsible change that we witness today is as much due to a lack of courage and trust and the presence of self-preserving fear as it is to other stated altruistic motives. As the scripture scholar, Eugene LaVerdiere, remarked in an article on fundamentalism, that issue is a personal problem arising from an immature trust development.

The fixation of the superego with individual acts militates against seeing the broader picture. Therefore, it renders any process of interpretation of law, etc. virtually impossible. Slowly but surely, it produces a 'tunnel vision' of reality. It turns trivialities into major issues. In a very real sense, superego needs to keep reality limited in order to avoid too many inconsistencies. The process of tailoring down our experience to fit the system is well known in the realm of superego and indeed, in the priesthood. Whenever we act because we are afraid of what 'they' might think or say, whenever we act anxiously, it is a fair bet that we are being manipulated by our superego.

The treatment of superego has been extensive because of the belief that it is a very good tool for understanding a major contributing factor to some of the problems within the priesthood, and its contribution to priests being abused and in turn becoming abusers. We use superego for the best of reasons to get people to 'live up to the faith'. Like most of the greatest evils in history, it is perpetrated in the name of the greatest good! However, it is one of our greatest contemporary enemies; and it is placed where enemies work best, within the camp! It is my personal conviction that any valid reform must identify what and where the enemies are and then address them as we try to introduce the new.

By way of rounding off this segment, it must be noted that other writers use categories other than that of the superego to explain the underlying phenomenon. Conrad Baars, for example, cites the 'fear emotion and the energy emotion'. The practical outcome of his theory is seemingly identical with that of men like Glaser and the moralists who follow him. My own preference for the superego explanation is because of its familiarity; and because it seems to coincide more accurately with my understanding of the treatment of discernment as given in the traditional spiritual writers.

Again, the important thing is the factual situation. A theory is only our way of understanding those facts, and the facts from my vantage point seem to be very clear.

Conversion and Dying

Life as Journey

One of the most significant documents that has come to us in the Church in recent times is the *Rite of Christian Initiation of Adults*. One of its special values is that it ritualises the Christian life as a *journey*. We are a pilgrim people, always on the way and living in tents, not fixed abodes. A rediscovery of this has been one of the most liberating things for many priests! The spiritual masters have always recognised the journey and they sought to spell out both the context of the various stages and the ways in which we should exercise ourselves in those stages. While this has always been in our tradition, it has not always been a realisation of the world cultures in which we live nor of the Church herself. For many of us, this tradition was treated very inadequately in seminary days: the format of the purgative, illuminative and unitive ways, or the degrees of beginner, proficient, and the perfect, are words that are known to us but are not much more than words!

Dangers

There are many reasons for this loss of spiritual insight. Some of them are historical and are rooted in the reactions to various heresies that threatened the Church at different times of her history. Some of the reasons are sociological and arise out of our worldview. For example the institutionalised understanding of Church finds it very difficult to deal with the whole question of change, especially changes in the personality or life style of its members. After all, unless the individual is the same yesterday, today and forever, how can we rely on him or her to perform the role and organise the task? Stability is a big value for the institutionalised model and the consequent spirituality that goes with it.

It is true that we are socialised both in the world at large and in the Church to believe that while there may be many different ages and stages in moving through childhood, existence in adulthood is one of plateau sameness. In fact, there are more ages and stages in adult existence than there are in the development throughout childhood. The impression that we arrive at maturity and simply continue on in a fixed stage is very convenient but quite wrong. Uniformity and sameness can be very much treasured by an organisation but they are not good for individuals. In fact, such an understanding of adult life can be very dangerous.

Responses

Almost universally, priests of my era have been taught prayer forms in the meditation mode that are appropriate to the beginning stages but inappropriate at later times. Without an awareness of the growth process, we come to find that what we began with is no longer fruitful. Because of superego guilts, some continue on doggedly; the wise bail out, and in some instances are lucky enough to find new forms – however, there can still remain residual guilt. Because of the myth we have learnt that change is not part of life, priests invariably will think that all has blown up. This is especially true when those crises or conversion points are accompanied by 'dark night' experiences where the feeling is that the bottom has fallen out of life. Too many men, not realising what is going on at such times, probably leave the active ministry altogether, or settle for a 'comfortable mediocrity' as they experience continued 'labour' but no birth. Again, we must realise that there are two ways of leaving priesthood: one is to leave and move out, the other is to leave and stay in! Figures on so-called 'defections' should really take account of both movements, although it would not be easy to apply criteria to measure the numbers who leave and stay-in. Maybe levels of contentment could be applied!

Help

Then again, when these major conversion phases are upon us we need help. Spiritual direction is essential for the first movements that encompass the 'dark night of the senses'. Providence seems to have decreed that we walk with our hand joined to another; as if to learn through necessity that faith is truly communal! Sadly, the meeting of this very important need is made more difficult for at least two reasons. First, the mind-set of the perfectionist model and the inevitable feelings of 'shame' and 'guilt' that accompany this call to journey. They militate against speaking out, even to a confidant. Secondly, there is not a group of people trained in the ways of the Spirit who are readily available to help. The priest is a spiritual director if he is anything, yet our training has not equipped us in this basic role. Something needs to be done about this, especially as the laity are looking to us more and more for just this service. All too often, at times of crisis, the advice given by friends, with the best of intentions, is not helpful. Phrases like 'don't worry about it', 'forget it', 'we all feel like that at times', 'go and have a good break and all will be well' etc. are at best useless and more often than not they are killing. Killing is not too strong a word because what is in operation is a birth process, which calls us through pain, labour and dying to new life. When that process is denied or blocked by certain 'common sense' myths, abortion of the birth or growth process can easily take place. As we often say, abortion is killing – and wherever it takes place.

Dying and rising to new life are central patterns to the living of the Christian life: "I wish to know Christ and the power flowing from his resurrection; likewise, to know how to share in his sufferings by being transformed into the pattern of his death. Thus do I hope that I may arrive at resurrection from the dead" [Philippians 3:10-11].

Living by Dying

In my years as a priest we have made a great, if challenging, advance in rediscovering the positive message contained in the Resurrection and its impact for us in daily living. However, alongside this we have not placed a fruitful theology or understanding of the central symbol of our faith – which is the cross. Again as always, there are many reasons that explain this.

Social Factors

For example, we live in the midst of a death-denying society and we are the children of our times even if we are also members of a Church which should save our brothers and sisters by being counter-cultural to such movements as deny death. The sort of gospel comment, reflected by a man like Ernest Becker in the title to his Pulitzer Prize-winning work, *The Denial of Death* [1974], is a teaching for all of us. The culture that surrounds us is one that denies death, and correspondingly has little place for a spirituality of the cross. We too share in this situation and while we have benefited by the refining of the Resurrection as an event of greater richness and meaning than the almost exclusively apologetic role it formerly had, we may well have made this gain at the cost of losing a healthy theology of the cross.

Spiritual Underdevelopment

This loss of sight of the cross obviously causes all kinds of aberrations in our personal living and in our pastoral practice. To name one example; how difficult is it for us to bury practices, programs or institutions that have died? We find it very difficult – because to admit that they have died feels like having to admit failure or that we are losing ground. No one lost more of this kind of ground than Jesus!

Child-focus

Linked up with this is the fact that we are in this country a Church that has dedicated itself almost exclusively to a pastoral program that aims to educate our children. It has been estimated roughly that something like 80% of our financial and staff resources are engaged in the partial education of less than 50% of our pre-adult members. The achievements in this area have been magnificent but there have been costs. We do not have any adequate adult education programs comparable to the sophistication of our school system. We teach faith to children and basically leave them with that faith and the accompanying theology to negotiate the changes and growth stages of adult life. Unless they remain children in some real and damaging sense, this process will not work.

However, it is true that if we do keep them in this childish mode and manage also to keep them on side, then it is easier for us to handle and manipulate them! There is another Catch 22 here – because as long as we treat them as children, they will act like children and expect to be 'cared for' and to have their needs met immediately as children do. As our numbers in the priesthood fall and the need to provide responsible lay ministers rises, we need more and more responsible adult laity who, rather than making demands, will be able to share the burden.

To bring about this necessary state of affairs, a mass conversion is needed; and who is going to shepherd them through it? Such a conversion implies conversion in the 'sheep', amongst the shepherds and also in our institutions; there is a lot of dying involved in such a program! Unless we have a healthy understanding of the call to share in the dying of Christ as distinct from 'dying full stop', we will never get to first base. I recall a saying of Dietrich Bonhoeffer claiming that to accept to be an apostle is to accept the call to die. It is important that any death be 'in Christ', that is, be a Spirit-filled call to die – only such dying is life-bearing. Unless we can discern the different deaths that surround us, we will never know when to die and when to fight. And unless we learn as priests to handle our inner feelings and movements, we will never be able to discern this central question of daily living. It is this need to discern the dying and rising of Christ in our daily ministry that is proposed as one of the key issues for priestly renewal by the American document, *The Spiritual Renewal of the Priesthood*, as we have already noted. Only adults can discern, because discernment requires maturity.

Achieving change

Against all that has been said above, a realistic note has to be recorded. To expect the needed conversion to happen to each and every one of the flock in order for the renewal I propose is clearly unreal. I incline to the proposition of Ken Wilber that a success rate of 5% amongst the leadership could be enough; and from there others will breath the new air into life.

In the context of the ways of journeying through the life we live, there are innumerable maps given in the great spiritual tradition that is ours. The 'mansion' image of St Teresa, the 'degrees of love' used by St Bernard, the 'four categories' of St Frances de Sales, are but some examples. Modern developmental psychologists have added greatly to this list of maps.

Jim Fowler spells out six faith patterns that seem to describe the situation of contemporary faith development. Here again, there is a startling coincidence with what seems to come through in our profiles. Fowler sees many adults as fixed into what he describes as Synthetic - Conventional Faith. Such faith would roughly correspond more to Model A-type spiritualities as described above. His work is illuminating. Without needing to canonise these authors, it seems critical that the type of information that they have to offer be part and parcel of the working knowledge of the contemporary parish clergy and that they be aware of how it relates to the writers in our tradition.

Affectivity

As a final word in this section, a word on affectivity is in order. Protective myths stand out everywhere to protect our systems from the nuisance value of letting people get in touch with their inner world and its workings.

Resistance

Our profiles depict priests as having a highly developed resistance to what they would term introspection or talking about their feelings. Experience would suggest that this resistance is more developed in priests than in other sections of the community. This can be traced to many sources, such as our philosophical training, our perfectionist model of spirituality, the reaction against the Liberal Protestant focus on experience that flowed into Modernism, etc. Whatever the cause, it is an incredible disability. Without the ability and readiness to grapple with inner experiences, conversion in the true sense of the word, the conversion that brings us to know the person of Christ and follow him, as distinct from following an ideology of some sort, is impossible. The way into the heart, 'the inner room' which is the place of prayer [Matthew 6:6], calls for the inner journey to be travelled as the way of coming to know self. This requires our being more and more 'at home with' our feelings and deeper inner movements. It means, especially, being in touch with our negative movements – or that part of our being that Jung described as the 'shadow'.

Then again, our inability to handle our inner reality and come to know self renders it impossible for us to adequately relate to others and to receive the support and affection that we need to live. Our fear of being found to be vulnerable will inevitably mean that we will not be able to establish warm and nourishing relationships. There is a Catch 22 involved here too. We need such relationships; but we cannot readily enter into them because we fear that, if people get too close, they might find out who we fear we really are! Yet to escape from that inhibiting fear, we need to be loved for ourselves by others.

Mercy

It would seem that the break-through from a servant/master type of relationship with the Lord, or with anyone else for that matter, only comes through an experience of mercy. Mercy, I believe, is that very important aspect of love wherein we experience love and acceptance from another while feeling at the same time our own 'unlovable side'. The move of our recent popes to focus on mercy is both striking and challenging. It is precisely in this that God proves his love for us: that "while we were still sinners, Christ died for us" [Romans 5:8].

Pope John Paul II pointed to the centrality of mercy in his 1980 Encyclical Letter, *Dives in Misericordia*. Amongst other instances, he cited the story of the Prodigal Son as the great parable of mercy - as it is also the great parable of conversion and of the Christian journey. It is in this parable that we see portrayed the 'two brothers' who reside within us all. There is a common-enough type of spirituality that has great difficulty in recognising the younger brother as the hero! The elder brother who will not give hospitality to the wandering younger brother can easily reflect a streak within us all that stands in the way of self forgiveness – which is a prerequisite for all forgiveness. Then again, we have the incredible story of the servants hired at the eleventh hour, as told in Matthew 20:1-16, and the challenging Psalm 123: "To you I lift up my eyes, to you who are enthroned in heaven. Behold, as the eyes of servants are on the hands of their masters, as the eyes of a maid are on the hands of her mistress, so are our eyes on the Lord, our God, till he have pity on us [donec misereatur nostri]".

Accountability

"The incarnation of Christianity implies a harmonious solution to the problem of the relations between the individual and the collective." [Simone Weil]

Before I conclude these reflections, a word on accountability seems appropriate. It was stated earlier that the 'felt experience', as one stands in the immature Model A mode of spirituality and faces the call of conversion to move on, can cause problems. As the Gospel warns us, we will be tempted to feel that such a move towards freedom and life will lead us to anarchy or a laissez-faire type of existence. Such an impression seems to be inevitable. There is no way to be moved along, or graced with new life, that does not involve us in the dying to former ways and the taking of 'risks': "For whoever wants to save their life will lose it, but whoever loses their life for me and for the gospel will save it" [Mark 8:35; Luke 9:23-26; 17:33; John 12:25]. In Matthew's presentation of this logion, there is the interesting reflection on the necessary readiness to stand out against father, mother, etc. and to make a man's enemies those of his own household [Matthew 10:34-39].

Adult Insight

There is no way of taking a full conversion journey that will not involve us in the feeling that we are abandoning virtue! Indeed, there will come a time when we begin to see virtue in our vices and vices in our virtues. As we begin to understand such intricacies of the faith journey and its dynamics, it becomes ever clearer that Christianity is truly an adult religion and that all about it cannot be appropriately proclaimed in its totality to the young; nor can a catechesis appropriate for the young be adequate for adults.

Priestly Insight

It is also true that not all of this journeying is a gift bestowed upon all: "My ways are not your ways', says the Lord"[Isaiah 55:8]. However, it is a fair presumption that those who are called to be leaders in the life of faith will also be called to be conversant with the ways the journey can develop. Such familiarity will best be obtained, not just from a theoretical knowledge, but from the experience of the actual journey. The disciple will surely lead like the Master who said, "Come and see" [John 1:38-39]. Experience would suggest that most priests, if not all, are in fact called along such a journey. Many of us sadly find ourselves 'punctured' along the side of the road or shacked up in some inn along the way because we do not have either map or guide!

Learnt through experience

Such an abandonment of what is deemed precious and important will only really be discovered as one moves over from one level of growth to another. We would all sympathise with the followers of Jesus who wanted to know in advance what was going to happen before they stepped out. To their reasonable question, "Rabbi, where do you stay?", Jesus answered, "Come and see" [John 1:38-39]. Strangely enough, it seems that priests are more prone to ask this type of question than the average person. However, for all of us, the answer of Jesus is the only one given; there is no other!

Only when we take the journey will we 'know' that in fact nothing of real worth or value has been lost. What was good in the old will still be there; however, it will now be better. "The reign of God is like a dragnet thrown into the lake, which collected all sorts of things. When it was full they hauled it ashore and sat down to put what was worthwhile into containers. What was useless, they threw away... Have you understood all this? ...Every scribe who is learned in the reign of God is like the head of a household who can bring from his storehouse both the new and the old" [Matthew 13:47-52].

The journey, however much of it we are called to make, will always be in the direction of greater trusting love in Jesus as Lord of our life [Acts 10:36]. It will always be away from our false idols and towards greater faith [Deuteronomy 5:6-7; Philippians 3:9].

Order and control

What I am advocating here is not a prescription for any form of anarchy or laissez-faire existence. As much as anyone, and maybe more than most, I would argue for the need of order and control for any organisation that is to operate responsibly and efficiently. Amongst other things, that is what the Church is called to be. The real question is the way we bring about that order and control. Clearly any exercise of power that operates by manipulating the inner life of persons is diabolical and against our most sacred teachings. "The truth cannot impose itself except by virtue of its own truth, as it makes its entrance into the mind at once quietly and with power" [*Dignitatis Humanae*, 2]

Yet this imposition of truth and order is what we can try to do, and from the evidence available, what we have done and are still doing. Such a use of power is insidious. In its place, we priests must set up criteria for accountability that are arrived at through corporate consensus and discernment amongst the presbyterate as a whole. The control and order that are necessary should come from our calling of each other to responsibility according to such established criteria. The actual details of how such a practice would be worked out are really beyond the scope of this work, but they would not involve us in any over-difficult exercise. Such a system of accountability has already been proposed to us in much of the papal documentation of recent years. It should serve well the needs of the corporate body and at the same time preserve the inner sanctuaries of the individual. Such structures would be 'out in the light' and not hidden in the realms of 'darkness'.

In actual fact, we would argue for greater structures of accountability and evaluation for ourselves as priests and for the laity as well. Too often because of the hidden nature of the existing controls, we feel that we are acting in a vacuum. Positive feedback and constructive evaluations and criticism, which must always go together, are not given. It is as if we had allowed a situation to arise that is beyond our control – this, of course, is always the case with 'evil spirits'.

The enemy within

In truth, our fight against superego-like guilts, used as a means of control and training, is a fight against the enemy that threatens the very fabric of the Church and of our Christian lives. It has been suggested that the real enemy of the Church today is not the enemy 'out there' but the enemy 'within'. In the context of what I am proposing here, it would seem that there is more than a modicum of truth in such an assessment!

Epilogue

Before I close, aware of the use of models in this work, let me say again that they are only instruments to help us understand the great mystery that is life and in which we share. The mystery will always lie beyond any expression a particular model supplies, and ultimately is only revealed in prayer.

I encourage the reader to leave behind anything that I have offered that is not helpful – but not before exposing it to prayer.

The following poem is one of many from the pen of Dr Eric Seal, a psychiatrist and layman who worked with us on the Humanita Board and whose wisdom and holiness all who knew him came to appreciate. I offer it here as a prayer to conclude this chapter and as a tribute to him.

Prayer

Is mind a tablet for God's signature
Designed? A mirror to reflect His love?
Creation's pinnacle evolved to prove
The power of the Creator, and ensure
Acknowledgment and awe, that should
Endure while reason rules?
No, mind is not a groove or channel to
Salvation. It must move in faith towards
God past reason's bright allure.
Humbled in prayer the human mind is
 Freed to reach past self, past ritual,
 Beyond the finitude of reason, past the
Need for satisfaction, so it may respond to
Love and Goodness. Like the seed in sod
Submerged, it grows to dialogue with God.

Eric Seal

Appendix 1

The experience of being a priest in Australia today

This document was presented to the Australian Catholic Bishops Conference during a day-long discussion on the Pastoral Care of Priests, which took place in Sydney on 28 November 1984.

From the discussion, the decision was taken to officially invite the American Centre for Human Development to establish the Ministry to Priests Program here in Australia.

Pilgrim Church

To be a priest today is to share with the entire People of God the call to be a pilgrim. To be a pilgrim is to be on a journey and - by definition - the journey is a long one. Now while journeying is an integral part of our history as God's People, it is not a familiar experience, coming as it does at the end of an unusually long period of stability. Nor is it an easy experience. The Exodus Story reminds us that our journeying always takes us into the desert – there to be reformed for life in a new land that awaits us somewhere in the future.

Today, I believe, we are still in the early days of our journey and it's not surprising that our common experience as priests is an experience of being in the desert – with all the connotations that this image carries in our Sacred History.

Differing Approaches to Priestly Life

Yet, within this common experience of desert, there are different specific experiences which arise from the varying ways that we adapt to the journey. For the sake of this presentation today, I would like to nominate three such distinct experiences.

1. *Advancing.* Firstly, there is the experience of a group of Australian priests who are well aware of where they are on the journey. These men have leaders who authenticate that things are in a state of change, and give permission to move in new directions. With a certain sense of excitement, they experience the God-given call to rebuild his dwelling place amongst men. Sure - these men are in some pain and they are undergoing the purifications that belong to any conversion process. But they are in good spirits because they see the death that they are undergoing as a redemptive death and they know the truth of the Gospel when it speaks of "sweet yokes and light burdens" [Matthew 11:30]. This group is well aware that the time of finding meaning, truth, and reality outside of themselves in institutions and structures has mostly gone. They accept this as a call to greater life and freedom – a call to simplify their lives and find their God more in the inner temple of their own hearts and the hearts of those who walk beside them on the journey. Generally, these men are men of hope, men of trust and, above all, men of patience. They are men who have found some kind of faith community where these all-important virtues are ministered to them. They see that risk-taking is important; and that mistakes can well become graces if only we admit to them and own our poverty. Available evidence would suggest that this group could number somewhere in the vicinity of 450 priests or 20% of the diocesan clergy. In general, we would have to say they are in good shape and they are doing a very constructive job.

2. *Holding back.* There is a second group of maybe similar size. Their experience is different. These men are more or less blind to the reality of where we are on the journey. Some of them haven't moved away from the situation which is the modern equivalent of Egypt in the Exodus Story. Others have

moved – but in the face of the hardships of the desert, they have changed their minds and are busy back-tracking towards Egypt! In some instances this group is in fairly high spirits. They still find supporters who affirm and applaud their stance. However, in my vision, I see these men as escapists – men who are living unrealistically.

3. *Confused.* A third group account for the remaining 60% or so of the priestly population – about 1400. I see them as being in varying stages of confusion and uncertainty. These men see the life of yesteryear as a thing of the past; but they do not have the categories to fully understand nor the ways to survive the new existence of the desert. Without such understanding and ways of coping, they are unable to live as true desert travellers. They are unable to negotiate the journey of conversion that we are all being called to as Church. Unable to adequately relax and take time out to regain their bearings, in many instances these men are overburdened with baggage from the past and unable to let go of so many time-conditioned beliefs and practices. Many in this group still see things and have the same expectations as when they were living in Egypt! It's easy for them to succumb to the temptation of the Golden Calf. Seeing the desert experience as a problem to be solved, they can run about frantically latching onto any new idea and trying to come up with instant answers. Because of their confusion, much of their ministry may be motivated more from their need to minister than from real needs of the people. To borrow another image from the Scriptures, these men are trying to pour new wine into old wineskins. Generally this group is highly anxious, prone to depression, and in real danger of burn-out. They are desperately in need of help – help to find their footing and support as they undergo the journey of conversion. Men in this category have been greatly helped by the program offered at the St Peter Centre.

Comparisons

In nominating these three groups and daring to place numbers on them, I am relying heavily on information that comes through various surveys carried out around the world and, in a beginning way, here in Australia. Whenever such surveys of priests are carried out, the resulting profiles are remarkably similar. I see no cause for surprise in this as I suspect that the basic problems confronting priests are mainly system ones, and the nature and shape of the system have been much the same world-wide.

If there is a place to make comparisons from country to country, there are real indications that the anxiety level of the Australian priest is higher than that of our American brothers. If true, this interesting observation could be due in part to the energy and dedication with which we have given ourselves to the patterns and attitudes of the past. It is an interesting fact of the spiritual life that those who have worked hardest in a previous "way" always find the desert experience more intense.

Whatever of this, there can be no question regarding the basic dedication and generosity of the Australian priest – which ever group he may belong to. From the beginning and into the present, we, I believe, are second to none; and the achievements of our Australian Church are admired worldwide. This, I'm sure, we would all readily acknowledge with due pride.

Professional Confirmation

Before continuing with a more detailed profile, I would like to quote from a presentation made by the psychiatrist, Conrad Baars, to the Bishops gathered in Rome for the 1971 Synod on the Priesthood. Conrad Baars writes: "Everyone agrees that there exists a crisis in the priesthood. Not everyone realises that this crisis… amounts to an illness, severe in some, moderate to slight in others… (Priests) suffer so acutely in their need for identity, self-worth, self-love and being loved... (They suffer from) a sense of powerlessness, normlessness, meaninglessness, self-estrangement and isolation".

In general, says Baars, "we estimate that 10-15% of all priests in Western Europe and North America are mature; 20-25% have serious psychiatric difficulties, especially in the form of neuroses and chronic alcoholism, or a combination of both; and 60-70 % suffer from a degree of emotional immaturity, which does not prevent them from exercising their priestly function but precludes their being happy men and effective priests whose fundamental role is to bring people to the joy of Christ's love and be the appointed affirmers of men."

Baars goes on to say: "We have been advised by Vatican observers of the crisis in the entire world Church that there is a remarkable agreement between their statistics and our percentages".

In brief, from my own experience and observations, from consultation and the results of psychological testing generally available to me, I suggest that the statement of Conrad Baars is also a fairly accurate description of the Australian priesthood.

Present Situation

You will notice that in making this statement I have moved away from the word 'experience' and used the word 'description'. I do this for the sake of precision because many priests are simply not consciously aware of their experience in this regard. Such an 'out-of-touchness' with emotions and feelings is in itself a serious concern; and amongst other things it is a reason why many express an appearance of contentment in the face of what I believe is the real situation. Before focusing on specific details, I affirm my conviction that the main problem areas hinge around the questions of power and affectivity.

As already mentioned, the above sources suggest very high anxiety levels and a high risk of burn-out amongst a majority of Australian priests. In many instances, this anxiety seems to be linked with abnormal guilts flowing from an over-idealised image of what one should be as a priest and/or repressed anger at being overpowered and trapped by expectations. Many of us have been so strongly socialised into the previously existing system that we are hardly able to act in healthy isolation from a system. Probably less than half of us are consistently capable of independently motivated behaviour that is the fruit of a free and mature conscience. This factor in itself leads to a sense of drivenness and gives rise to great tension and frustration.

Test material and experience with direction indicate that for many the stage of personality development is that of an identification with our role rather than a true personal identity. This is further complicated when we find ourselves 'pressed' into a role that no longer provides satisfaction or feelings of self-worth. It's true that satisfaction with self and with ministry is generally poor. Whenever the opportunity arises, I invite priests to rate priestly morale on a scale from 1 to 10. More often they will score it around 3 or 4. Very few will score it above 5! In many instances, our emotional development is more consistent with that of late adolescence or early adulthood.

Whenever stories are told, a large number of Australian priests express unresolved anger from their seminary training where they feel that their emotional life and relational abilities were stultified rather than nourished. Our level of basic trust is low; and we find it difficult to delegate and to trust others – especially the laity!

For so many, there is an urgent need for authorities to give positive encouragement and a form of clear permission before we are able to move out on the journey of change and conversion at all. If we are to understand and personally integrate current movements in the Church, there is a widespread need for theological updating in the context of conversion.

For the most part, in-service training hasn't faced the fact that, deep down, the need is for conversion and not simply the giving of new ideas or skills. Such conversion calls for a ministry not only to the mind but to the whole person. There is a serious lack of confidence and formation in the matter of personal prayer and much – much – undue guilt in the matter of prayer.

For many of us, the scriptures remain a closed book. Maybe it is not unconnected with this fact that our preaching is felt to be poor and, judged by the majority of the people in the pews, to be poor.

Because we lack the ability to handle inner experience and are suspicious of feelings, especially those of a negative nature, we are not at all at home in the dynamics of discernment. Our spirituality is often coloured with Pelagian or semi-Pelagian overtones; and getting things right is seen as more important than faith and trust in the unconditional love that our merciful God offers to us. Because we haven't received an adequate understanding of the Church's rich teaching on the spiritual life, we are very vulnerable in the face of our own history and the contemporary expectations of growing numbers of the laity. Good spiritual directors are hard to find; and, generally, we do not feel competent to give such direction to others. Almost universally, the dynamics of the spiritual journey or spirituality are poorly known, and the normal ebbs and flows in that journey are dangerously misinterpreted. From a general vocational point of view, the psychological profiles of many show men more suited to work with things than with people.

Many are 'loners' and find social gatherings and group work difficult. They prefer to work on a one-to-one basis but not at a deep or intimate level. In fact, many appear to be quite obstructive in group situations – especially group situations with the laity.

While there is a desperate need for affirmative feed-back, the fear of rejection and the possibility of being hurt lead us to avoid feed-back or evaluation all together. We are oversensitive; and the mistaken belief that no feed-back is better than negative feed-back isolates us excessively. We badly lack adequate structures of affirmation and of accountability.

Healthy supportive friendships are rare, even though many of us are well-skilled in the techniques of relating. The inability to share and to confront others in a constructive way are amongst the main obstacles to such relationships. Perhaps it is in the area of relationships more than anywhere else that the contemporary Australian priest experiences most difficulty. This difficulty becomes more acute as we view the Church increasingly in the image of a people in communion. Our contemporary ecclesiology challenges us at those points where we are especially vulnerable. If we are to continue to protect such areas of vulnerability, it will be only at a great cost to the renewal of the Church called for in Vatican II.

In the area of relationships, we are caught in a Catch 22 situation. The breakdown of the structures means that we need warm, fruitful relationships in order to survive and indeed to minister. And we need to find them amongst both men and women. However, to experience such relationships, one has to begin to gamble a little dangerously with many of the values that were propagated by the previous system and begin to engage in processes of self-disclosure and a type of sharing based more on equality than from a basis of power or superiority.

So much that belonged to the behaviour recommended in the previous understanding of Church and priesthood militates against this – and so the priest feels caught. One part of us wants something desperately while another part prohibits us from taking the steps to achieve what we so dearly desire. The common experience of loneliness poses profound questions for our celibate lifestyle because we lack the inner resources to handle this loneliness constructively.

Another related Catch 22 situation exists in the area of power and authority. The call of the post Vatican II Church is clearly towards a more democratic and participatory style of government. However, because of our emotional development, many of us find it difficult to delegate or take up this shared responsibility when it is offered. In many instances, we react quite erratically when such responsibility is given. One part of us desperately needs to have autonomy and creative scope while another part of us seems to baulk at challenging burdens and additional possibilities for failure.

While there seems to be a growing impatience with authority, in many instances we seem to prefer to leave the responsibility with the Bishop and then have the added luxury of a scapegoat to blame when things do not go smoothly. We are often quite impatient, and handle ambiguity and tension [and those things we would generally lump under the heading of the cross] with difficulty. In general, we are more likely to react than to respond when faced with difficult situations. This may well be the result of a feeling that we have been badly done by in the past. Certainly, it is true that available psychological profiles indicate that we perceive ourselves as men who have been hurt in the past by excessive demands made on us both by ourselves and by others.

From experience with test profiles undertaken by a number of Australian priests, a psychologist offered to suggest the following statement of needs:

- "There is a need for growth from inadequate conceptual frameworks that are over-idealistic and unreal.
- The priests need to have structures to administer affirmation and evaluation – for themselves and their work.
- Mutually agreed upon accountability structures would seem to be essential.

- Group work would be needed to administer peer help and self-help.
- Few of the men have access to ongoing interpersonal support – as opposed to social support.
- There is need for a great deal of self-image development.
- Tension management techniques are necessary if the buildup of tension to dangerous levels is to be avoided. Such tension, if unattended, could well lead to psychosomatic illnesses or inappropriate behaviour of one form or another.
- The need to move out of role-determined behaviour for recreation is important.
- Permission for change needs to be provided by the respected authorities."

Conclusion

In conclusion, I want to say that in attempting to paint a picture of the Australian priest in so short a time, I have felt the need to be painfully selective. The choice to focus on our more pressing needs as the most helpful way to contribute to this forum has not allowed me to acknowledge the positive steps that have already been taken to provide support and assistance. In arguing that more is needed, I do not want to appear to be critical of what is already underway. The establishment of the St Peter Centre and the efforts to make it succeed, along with the fact of this day, are but two examples that show that we are responding and responding with zeal.

From my personal experience, I must say that the readiness of the Church as a whole to rally in support of priests is remarkable. Somehow we seem to know their personal worth and their sincerity and their importance for any real renewal in the Church. Nor do these presented needs that I've touched on place unmanageable demands on us. I believe an appropriate and adequate response is well within our grasp. Hopefully, what I have said will be of some real assistance in helping us to do what we so clearly want to do.

Appendix 2

A final reflection

From my earliest years, I am aware of my preoccupation with the question 'what will I do?' From early on my answer was a priest and as a kind of fallback position I saw myself as an engineer, a civil engineer.

As long as I remember, I saw myself as something of a maverick. I would describe this as being ever uneasy with how things were and looking for something more, a kind of feeling that there was more to come. As I fantasised as an engineer, I took hold of the story of the retired Irish plumber who on his first overseas trip was transfixed at Niagara Falls and could not be coaxed to leave. Eventually, when challenged with the inevitably question as to what was the matter, he enthusiastically replied, "You know, I think I can fix it." Somehow, that story touched into my psyche; and my image of myself as an engineer was that of a forensic engineer, that is, someone who examined structures that had failed and were not performing properly to discover the causes and find a remedy.

Priesthood

Well, I became a priest and not an engineer; and from my first years in ministry my maverick streak was at work leading me to look for what was missing and what was not working. As I look back on my life now in its closing days, I am amazed at how and where what I am calling my maverick streak has led me, and almost always against my expectation. Without giving chapter and verse of my history, allow me to note the statement of my beloved mentor, Father Jim Gill SJ, who once said that few had a wider experience of priesthood than I had! Of course, all of these aspects of my life have provided the warp and the woof of what has become a journey of both agony and ecstasy. It has been a journey, and on many levels: geographically, emotionally, intellectually, socially and spiritually; and it still goes on. As I touch back into it now, I see a journey assisted by others, yet often hindered by those within my Church community who, I dare to believe, always wanted to help!

Since the mid-70s, when I joined with David Walker in establishing the Educational Centre for Christian Spirituality, I have been engaged in adult education; and, especially since 1980, with the education of priests. During my academic life, it has been my privilege to search with countless men and women of exceptional knowledge, wisdom and sanctity. It is from this source that I dare to share whatever I can for this current project.

Clergy Sexual Abuse

When the clergy sexual abuse scandal surfaced in the 90s, I was shocked. Yet I also realised that what I saw as a primary disease infecting our Church community and, within it, our priesthood – our special illness, if you like – was now out in the open and able to be treated.

For me, this special trauma of the abuse scandal appeared as a rock-bottom experience. Yet it engaged all the constituent factors and, with the grace of the Holy Spirit, provided an opportunity for a rebirth we have been struggling to embrace since Vatican II. Understandably, its appearance gave rise generally to shock, followed by anxious reactions, alongside of more balanced responses which came from the more thoughtful and perceptive who had been aware of the issues elsewhere for some time. Typically, my critical eye identified three stages in the response.

Bad apples

Stage One saw the issue in terms of bad apples who had managed to find their way into the ranks. These men would need to be eradicated and barriers put in place to prevent similar bad apples from entering in future. From my personal knowledge of brother priests and from my experience of working alongside reputable professionals, I was driven to believe that the number of bad apples was very few. The majority of offenders were more accurately seen as sick with illnesses which had a lot to do with the environment in which they had been living. These men and their condition became the focus of my attention as I reflected on the data upon which the thesis of this book is built. Most of us who entered seminaries and submitted to the process to ordination started with a similar dream, the dream to help people and save our souls. Those who have fallen by the wayside have not fallen on their own; and those of us who have been spared their shame know that 'there but for the grace of God go I'.

Faulty leadership

Stage Two of the reply came as those in positions of authority began to identify mistakes they had made in dealing with the perpetrators of abuse. For those who require a scapegoat in such circumstances [and who amongst us does not?], here was another way to respond to the challenge. Again, while I saw there were definitely contributing factors to be found in the failure of administrative leadership, I was confident that we had to look further.

> [At this point I would like to pause to reflect on a man who, I believe, suffered as much as anyone, and even more than most, in the midst of this battle. He was a bishop whom I know personally to have done more than any other bishop

I know to care for his priests, making his own the catch cry, 'Who cares for the carers?' Like others, he had his problem priests, actually more than most; and they tore his heart apart as he literally went to the ends of the earth seeking ways to help and to deal with them.

Along the way, he received advice from "experts", both ecclesiastical and secular, whose confidence in many cases far outweighed their competence; and he was encouraged to act in ways that are now seen to have been ineffectual. In true scapegoat style, he carried upon his shoulders the failings of his legal and medical advisors, along with those of his fellow bishops who have been all too ready to have him become the focus for bearing the corporate guilt of many. This man was particularly committed to justice and truth. Indeed, he had chosen as his episcopal motto, 'Doing the truth in love' – which indicated that this was the main focus of his life, and he was as committed to his flock as one could be. Some have seen his heart as more open for his priests than for their victims – but ultimately I don't think that this was possible, and the explanation for any seeming discrimination must be found elsewhere.

When I mention this man's name, you may find need to pause – such had been the power of the scapegoating mechanism that had operated in his regard. His story has played a big part in convincing me that our problem is not just bad apples or dumb bishops but a dysfunctional and abusive system. Yes, this man's name is Ron Mulkearns, and like us all he was not without fault.]

Systemic Failure

Back now to Stage Three, where my main concern is the ecclesiastical structure, and in particular the way it sets out to form and educate its membership. Let me note here that while my focus is specifically on priests and issues of clergy abuse, this issue of education applies universally within the Church and gives rise to a dysfunctional Church family.

When I look back on my time of ordination in 1963, I see myself as one who felt he had arrived and achieved a long pursued goal. Having applied myself assiduously to my years of training, I was confident that I had what was needed and was able to find out what I did not know! Of particular interest was the fact that I saw reality as an object, as something static. That observation fitted easily into the prevailing classical world view prevailing in the Church at the time. A major concern for my thesis is this objective view of reality and the static nature of life that was mine in 1963. Developmental psychologists had for years been speaking of ages and stages in our life growth, and charting their significance. Prior to their arrival, the spiritual writers had explored the same concepts, naming developmental ages and stages on one's spiritual journey. Even during our seminary years, the tradition of the spiritual masters, assisted by authors such as Vallgomera, Scaramelli, Garrigou-Lagrange and Tanqueray, to name a few, struggled to be heard.

I presume to suggest that more than a little of our spiritual tradition got lost in the cloud of fear and distress within which Church authorities shrouded the new discipline of psychology and the challenge posed by authors such as Freud. Still today, I have vivid memories of raising the issue of the stages and ways of the spiritual life with our professor, reputed to be an eminent Jesuit, who unmistakably made me feel that, here I was again, doing my maverick thing and going beyond the boundaries. In no uncertain terms, he told us - and me in particular - that we need not concern ourselves with such matters as neither ourselves nor those we would be called to minister to would ever find ourselves beyond the stage of beginners!

Recalling this incident now so many years later fills me with anger and disgust because, while that man was considered to be wise and learned, he was so much a captive of his time as to abuse his students with his treatment of the matter. I use the word 'abuse' because I see this as a prime example of what I will claim to be the damaging quality of a dysfunctional and abusive ecclesiastical system, which has contributed in a major way to the outbreak of abuse within the priesthood as it was educated and formed in those years.